THE STANDARD DEVIANTS STUDY SIDEKICK

THE ADVENTUROUS WORLD OF COLLEGE ALGEBRA PARTS 1&2 STUDY SIDEKICK – 1ST EDITION

Written by The Standard Deviants® Academic Team, including:
Dan Kalaman, Ph.D.
Karen Hanson
Bradley Zweig

Edited by:
Chip Paucek
Rachel Galvin

Contributing Editors:
Richard Semmler, Ph.D.
Jennie Halfant

Graphic Design by:
C. Christopher Stevens

800-238-9669
e-mail: cerebellum@mindspring.com
www.cerebellum.com

OTHER SUBJECTS FROM CEREBELLUM:

Printed in the beautiful U.S.A.

HOW TO USE THIS BOOK

CHECK OUT THE VIDEOS. Please notice the plural **videos**! This single workbook corresponds to two of our Video Course Reviews: The Adventurous World of College Algebra Parts 1 and 2. You'll be much better off if you buy and watch both tapes.

FOLLOW ALONG. The **VIDEO NOTES** section does your work for you! We've already taken all of your notes—all you have to do is follow along with the videos. We've even given you a **VIDEO TIME CODE** for both videos. Just reset your VCR counter to 0:00:00 when the Cerebellum logo appears at the beginning of each tape. These clocks `0:00:00` give you the time code for each important section so you know where to fast forward to! This will enable you to learn and retain material much more effectively. Just stop the tape after a difficult section and read through your notes!

Also, so you'll know which video we're talking about, we've put these markers in the upper right–hand corner: **V1** and **V2**. **V1** means you're in a section that covers material from The Adventurous World of College Algebra Part 1. **V2** means you're in a section that covers material from The Adventurous World of College Algebra Part 2.

LEARN NEW STUFF. Unfortunately, we just can't include everything about algebra in two videos. The **OTHER IMPORTANT STUFF** section gives other cool facts you'll need to ace your tests.

TEST YOURSELF. QUIZZES and **PRACTICE EXAMS** allow you to test yourself and make sure you've covered all the bases. The answers appear at the back–*don't cheat!*

HAVE FUN. The book is chock-full of diversions and stress relievers, and there are two of those neat flippy pictures on the bottom of each page.

TABLE OF CONTENTS

VIDEO TIME CODES

VIDEO NOTES

cerebellum
CORPORATION

TEST YOURSELF

TABLE OF CONTENTS

OTHER IMPORTANT STUFF

TEST YOURSELF

The Adventurous World of College Algebra Part 2

STRESS RELIEF

ANSWERS

The Adventurous World of College Algebra Part 1

TABLE OF CONTENTS

The Adventurous World of College Algebra Part 2

STUDY SIDEKICK

VIDEO TIME CODE

The Adventurous World of College Algebra Part 1

Bloopers

VIDEO NOTES

The Adventurous World of College Algebra Part 1

`0:04:25`

What is Algebra?

`0:04:30`

Section A: A Little History

Algebra is a sort of universal arithmetic that replaces numbers with letters. Next to geometry, algebra is the oldest form of mathematical study. Records written in ancient Egyptian, Arabic, and Chinese show that all of these cultures explored aspects of algebra. Algebra was developed to solve practical problems dealing with astronomy, architecture, and property.

Fortunately for us, the ancient Egyptians, Chinese, and Arabs did all the hard work in developing algebra. We just have to follow their lead. The English word "algebra" actually comes from the Arabic words "al jebr," meaning "the coming together of parts."

One of the most common purposes of algebra is "solving for x" or defining a variable. You'll spend most of your time in algebra and on your tests doing the same thing.

You can think of an algebra problem as a jigsaw puzzle with one piece that you know is missing. But just because you're missing a piece doesn't mean you can't put together the part of the puzzle you have. And once you've fit the pieces that you

12

do have together, you can see the size and shape of the missing piece, so you'll be able to recognize that piece when you see it. Finding that missing piece, the X variable, is the core of algebra.

So the object of algebra is the quest to discover the value of the unknown variable X.

Section B: Terminology

`0:07:18`

The basic building block for all of college algebra is the function.

⊙ A **function** is an algebraic statement that provides a link between two or more variables. It can be used to find the value of one of the variables if you know the values of the others. So, take the simple function:

$$y = 2x,$$

or, in words,

y equals 2 times x.

If you know x, you can find y…just like if you know Ernie, you can find Bert.

This situation occurs any time one variable appears by itself on one side of the equation. In

$$y = 3x + 4,$$

y is a function of x because y appears by itself. It is important that y is unadorned by other symbols:

it isn't y^2 or $\frac{1}{y}$ or $\sqrt{y}$; it's just plain y.

⊙   Whatever you compute using the other side of the equation just gives you the value of y. So in this way, a function is a codependent relationship between an x and a y:

without x, you can't get y.

That's the idea of a **function**.

Ooten gleten glopen globen.

–Def Leopard

Another way to think of a function is that it's a very specific kind of relation in which each element of one set is paired with one, and only one, element of a second set. Remember that a relation is any numerical expression relating one number, or set of numbers, to another.

There are basically two kinds of relations: **equations** and **inequalities**. Relations can be as simple as the equation:

$$1 + 3 = 4$$

or the inequality:

$$8 > 5$$

These specific numbers are being related to each other. The arithmetic you learned in grade school explored specific number relations.

Algebra explores relations between nonspecific numbers (or variables like x and y) which represent a whole set of possible numbers. Variable relations (expressions that contain variables, such as the equation $2x + 3 = 9y$) look more like the kind of algebraic expressions you've seen before.

When we said a function is a specific kind of relation, we were really thinking of equations and inequalities. What kinds of equations and inequalities? The kind that can be used to determine just one value for one of the variables.

That's exactly what we saw before with $y = 3x + 4$. When you substitute a value for x, you can calculate just one value for y. So the very specific kind of relation that qualifies as a function always boils down to this: an equation with one variable by itself on one side of the equal sign. And we say that the variable is a function of whatever variables appear on the other side.

Standard Deviant Hot Tip

Okay, you've probably seen this before:

$$f(x)$$

It stands for "function of x," but it gets repeated so often that to save time it's shortened to be written as $f(x)$ and pronounced as "f of x." $f(x)$ is just another way of saying y in a function. We'll explain.

It works like this:

⊙ Before, when we wrote $y = 3x + 4$, we expressed y as a function of x.

⊙ Another way of writing this is:

$$y = f(x) = 3x + 4,$$

or just

$$f(x) = 3x + 4.$$

This is how you'll see functions represented most often, so it's called the **standard form for expressing a function**. Functions are easiest to deal with when they are in standard form; most of college algebra is concerned with putting functions that are not in standard form into standard form, so you'll need to be really familiar with this kind of relation.

0:12:12

16

In algebra, be prepared to see equations like these:

$$f(x) = 2x + 1$$

$$g(x) = x^2 - 3x + 2$$

$$h(x) = 2^x$$

Each of these examples defines a function of x, and we use different letters (like f, g, and h) to distinguish between different examples. These functions are read as:

0:13:03

$f(x) = 2x + 1$ means "f of x equals two times x plus one."

$g(x) = x^2 - 3x + 2$ means "g of x equals x squared minus three times x plus two."

$h(x) = 2^x$ means "h of x equals two to the x power."

> **Remember: When you're given an equation for a function, you can calculate the function as soon as you know a value for x.**

⊙ For g, if you know that $x = 5$, you can immediately substitute $x = 5$ into the equation so

$$g(x) = x^2 - 3x + 2$$

$$g(5) = 5^2 - (3 \times 5) + 2$$

$$g(5) = 25 - 15 + 2$$

$$y = 12.$$

The right side of the equation shows how to do a specific calculation.

If it seems like we're spending a lot of time on what is really just vocabulary, that's because algebra, like most math, is written in a very precise, extremely specific language of its own. So, just like with any foreign language, it's incredibly important to know the vocabulary of algebra. For instance, if you went to Botswana, you would have to know the language of **Setswana**.

Anyway, you have to be familiar with some of the terminology we'll be using to discuss functions. If you already know this stuff, don't get impatient—just flip ahead to a topic you don't know!

`0:14:52`

In most situations, the standard form can be considered in terms of "terms" (har, har). When algebraic expressions are made up of parts that are added and subtracted, each part is called a **term**.

Terms are always separated by plus or minus signs.

For example, in the function:

$$f(x) = x^2 - 3x + 2$$

The three "terms" that make up this equation are x^2, $-3x$, and 2. In this first part of algebra, we will mainly look at terms that are made up of constants, variables, and powers. All of the terms in the preceding examples are composed that way.

18

⊙ Each term has two parts: a **constant** and a **variable**.

The **constant** is the number, which always has a constant (unchanging) value.

The **variable** is the letter, which has a value that varies.

In $f(x) = x^2 - 3x + 2$, each term has a variable x, raised to a different power.

The first term: x to the second power, or x squared, (x^2).

The second term: x to the first power, (x^1), or the x in $-3x$.

The third term: x to the zero power, (x^0), which equals 1.

The constant 2 is really 2 times x to the zero power. Since x^0 always equals 1, it's never seen but always there, kind of like air. The same thing applies to the term $-3x$; the x is raised to power of 1. It isn't seen, but it's always there.

A function or expression with only one term is called a **monomial**. Examples of monomials are

$$2 \qquad 3x^2 \qquad 5x^{12}$$

Expressions containing two terms are called **binomials**. Examples of binomials are:

$$x^2 + 2 \qquad 4x^4 + x^2 \qquad 5x^{12} + 3x^7$$

"Oh no!
It's ping
pong balls!"

-Captain Kangaroo

`0:17:52`

◉ **Trinomials**, then, are expressions with three terms.
Examples of trinomials are

$$8x^3 + x^2 + 2 \qquad 4x^4 + x^2 + 5 \qquad 5x^{12} + 3x^7 + x^3.$$

Other expressions with three terms:

"Tap the keg."

"Scrub my pony."

"Shave the ham."

Another very important word is **polynomial**. Any expression
or function containing one or more monomial, binomial,
trinomial, or basically any other nomial, is a polynomial.

Now, sometimes a polynomial may appear in disguise.

The expression

$$(3x - 2)(x + 4)$$

doesn't look like our earlier examples. It isn't made up of
simple terms separated by plus or minus signs, and it has
parentheses. But, as we will see, it can be put into a different
form.

If you multiply it out, $(3x - 2)(x + 4)$ becomes $3x^2 + 10x - 8$,
and can be recognized as a polynomial. So the word **polynomial** refers to anything that appears in, or can be put in, the form
of a monomial, binomial, trinomial, or any other nomial.

cerebellum

VIDEO NOTES

> The highest exponent in any polynomial is called the **degree** or the **order** of the polynomial.

⊙ For example, the function $f(x) = 8x^3 + x^2 + 2$ is a third-degree polynomial because the highest exponent in the equation is 3.

⊙ And the function $f(x) = 3x^7 + 5x^{12} + x^3$ is a twelfth-order polynomial because the highest exponent in the equation is 12.

The constants that are multiplied by the x variables in each term are called the **coefficients**.

In $3x^2$, 3 is the coefficient of x^2.

In $-5x^7$, -5 is the coefficient of x^7.

And in $64x^5$, 64 is the coefficient of x^5.

That covers the basic terminology we will use when discussing functions.

Quiz 1

1. A function is a relation in which each element of a set is paired with _____ element(s) of the second set.

2. A short way to write "the function of x" is _____.

3. The standard form for expressing a function is _____.

4. A "term" in mathematics has two parts, the _____ and the _____.

5. Any math expression or function containing one or more term is called a _____.

Functions

 `0:21:35`

Section A: Domain and Range

`0:21:56`

To evaluate or find the value of a function, you must substitute values for the variables. If you substitute, or plug in, certain values for x, you'll get a resultant set of values for y, or $f(x)$, like this:

In this example, let's evaluate the function

$$f(x) = 2x + 1.$$

And let's say that you have this set of numbers:

{–2, –1, 0, 1, 2, 3}.

⊙ Substituting each number in our set for x will give us a value in a second set, or the set of $f(x)$'s.

For example, substituting -2 for x gives us:

$$f(x) = 2x + 1$$
$$= 2(-2) + 1$$
$$= -3$$

⊙ Substituting $-2, -1, 0, 1, 2,$ and 3 into the function, we find that our second set is:

{– 3, –1, 1, 3, 5, 7}.

These two sets have specific names. The first set, the set of x values, is called the **domain**. The domain is also referred to as

DOMAIN
- set for the independent variable

the set for the **independent** variable, because this set of values is nonconditional. Each value of x does not depend on any other variables or constants in a function.

Now remember, a **function** is a relation in which each value of the domain is paired with one, and only one, value of the range. This pair of elements, one from the domain and one from the range, is called an ordered pair, and looks like this: (x, y).

The second set, the set of values that we found for $f(x)$, is called the **range**. The range is also known as the set for the **dependent** variable because each value of $f(x)$ depends on a value of x in the domain.

Remember: Each pair of elements, one from the domain and one from the range, is called an ordered pair and it looks like this:

$$\{x, f(x)\}$$

0:24:18

Section B: Graphs and the Coordinate Plane

As you may remember, ordered pairs can be plotted on a graph where the horizontal axis of the graph represents values for x and the vertical axis of the graph represents values for $f(x)$.

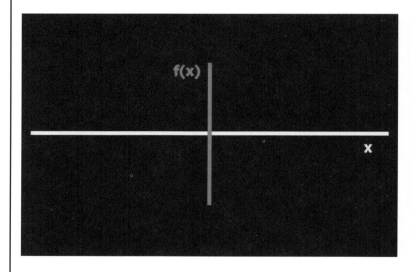

Using our function $f(x) = 2x + 1$, We can plug values from our domain $\{ -2, -1, 0, 1, 2, 3 \}$ into our function to get the range, or y values, of $\{ -3, -1, 3, 5, 7 \}$.

We can then plot these ordered pairs, or points, on the graph of our function.

$$(-2,-3)\ (-1,-1)\ (0,1)(1,3)\ (2,5)\ (3,7)$$

f(x)

x

$$f(x) = 2x+1$$
ordered pairs
(-2,-3),(-1,-1),(0,1),(1,3),(2,5),(3,7)

Of course, you've seen graphs before–but you're probably used to seeing the "$f(x)$" value written as a "y" value. Don't let this little ruse confuse you. They're the same thing. *So if it's easier for you to think of f(x) as y, then go ahead!*

After all, earlier we used y before we replaced it with $f(x)$. What's important is to remember that:

⊙ x is the domain, or independent variable, and is graphed on the horizontal axis.

STUDY SIDEKICK

⊙ $f(x)$, or y, is the range or dependent variable, and is graphed on the vertical axis.

In algebraic functions, the domain doesn't have to be made up of whole numbers; it can also include decimal or fractional values. So instead of considering only 2 and 3, we would also allow 2.87, $2\frac{2}{3}$, 2.222, and all the other possible numbers between 2 and 3 to fit in the domain. These whole numbers, fractions, and decimals (finite and infinite) are all referred to as **real numbers.**

There ARE numbers that aren't real. For historical reasons, they're referred to as imaginary numbers, although in philosophical terms they are real enough. We'll talk plenty about imaginary numbers later. For now, just think of real numbers as the numbers that get used in every day life: whole numbers, fractions, and decimals, including repeating decimals like .333333, which is what you get if you try to convert the fraction $\frac{1}{3}$ into an exact decimal.

There is another kind of number that goes on forever without repeating any pattern. The decimal portion of the number goes on forever without repeating itself, like 3.14159265359 etc. You probably recognize this number as pi (π).

These are called transcendental, or irrational, numbers. You night hear either of these names from mathematical specialists. The clue to transcendental numbers is that they can't be put in the form of a fraction and still be exact.

Surprisingly, there are actually more of these infinite nonrepeating decimals than there are of any other kind of real number.

They show up often as a result of solving equations in algebra. That means that many algebra problems do not have answers that can be stated exactly using fractions or normal (finite) decimals. Still, finite or infinite, all decimals are real numbers. A typical domain for a function might consist of:

⊙ All real numbers between 2 and 3.

⊙ All real numbers between −4 and 4.

⊙ All real numbers between any other pair of numbers.

There are an infinite number of real numbers in any such set, and they crowd infinitely close together, so graphing the function results in an infinite number of connected points. All these points plotted together will form a line or curve, which is the graph of the function. We'll get back to real numbers and graphs later. For now, let's look at a practical example of a function.

We're going to need a bigger boat.

-Roy Scheider

0:29:04

Section C: A Practical Example

Simon Wright, a bullwhip maker in "Ye Olde Bullwhippe Shoppe," can make two bullwhips in one day. At the start of the day, he has one bullwhip that he made yesterday. Business hasn't been very good lately, so assuming he does not sell any bullwhips, how many whips will Simon have by the end of the day? Three days from now? A week from now?

A simple function can be used to solve this problem. In this case, the function will be a relation between the number of days that have passed and the number of whips that Simon has.

We know that this morning, after 0 days, Simon has 1 whip. By the end of today, after 1 day, Simon will have the 1 whip he started with plus the 2 whips he made today, for a total of 3 whips.

Tomorrow night, after 2 days, he will have the 1 whip from yesterday, plus 2 whips from today, plus the 2 more whips that he will make tomorrow. So tomorrow night he'll have a total of 5 whips.

Following this same pattern, after 27 days the number of whips will be 1 plus 2 plus 2 plus 2 and so on for 27 twos.

That is, there will be 1 plus 2 times 27, which equals 55 whips. If we use the variable x to stand for the number of days, the pattern looks like this:

After x days there will be 1 plus $2x$ whips.

That sentence expresses the number of whips as a function of x, because as soon as the value of x is known, we can immediately compute the number of whips.

Using the standard form, we write

$$f(x) = 1 + 2x$$

where x is the number of days that have passed and $f(x)$ is the number of whips Simon has.

If three days have passed, then $x = 3$, and the number of whips is

$$f(3) = 1 + 2(3)$$

$$= 7.$$

So, in 3 days, Simon will have 7 whips.

If a year has passed, then:

$$x = 365$$

$$f(365) = 1 + 2(365)$$

$$= 731.$$

In a year Simon will have 731 whips (assuming he doesn't sell any) which, based on current whip trends, seems possible.

As we said, all functions can be graphed. By plotting all of the x and y values of Simon's function, we can see that it looks like this:

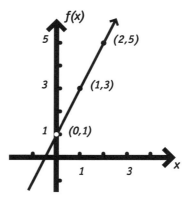

Now, sometimes when you do practical word problems like this, the domain is restricted by the meaning of the variable. In this case, it doesn't make sense for x to have a negative value, because x represents time in this equation

Video Notes

and time doesn't run backwards. So here, x is greater than or equal to zero. This is just another instance of real life interfering with algebra.

We know that a function is defined as a relation in which each value of the domain is paired with one, and only one, value of the range. So there is only one value for $f(x)$ that is paired with any given value of x. We can make sure that a graph is a function by using the **vertical line test**.

To start the vertical line test you set a vertical line on the graph and move it along the horizontal axis (the x-axis). We'll use the function of Simon's whip inventory to demonstrate.

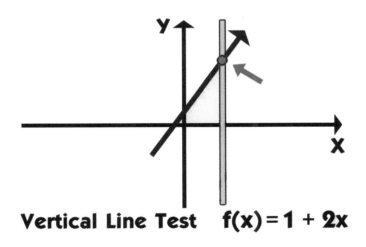

Vertical Line Test $f(x) = 1 + 2x$

"Move vertical line along horizontal axis"

As long as the line touches no more than one point of the graph of the equation, the graph is a function. But if it ever touches the graph of the equation at more than one point at any place on the graph, the graph is not a function.

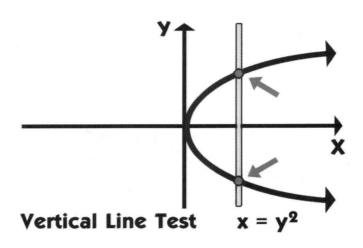

Vertical Line Test $x = y^2$

"Not a function"

VIDEO NOTES

Section D: Inverse Functions

We don't want to leave this introduction to functions without mentioning the concept of the inverse function. Thinking visually, inverting a graph means reversing the coordinates of each point on the graph.

⊙ For example, if (2,5) is one of the points on the original graph, (5,2) will be a point on the inverted graph.

⊙ If (3,7) is another point on the original graph…(7,3) will be another point on the inverted graph.

Here are some examples of graphs and their inverses:

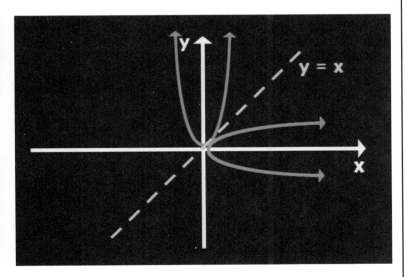

"From the video"

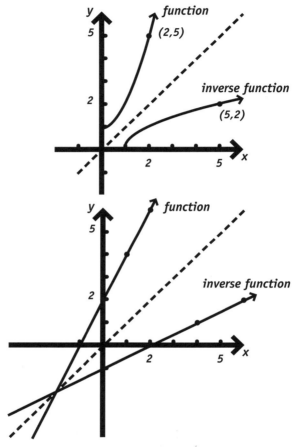

You can see that the original graph and the inverted graphs appear to be mirror images, with the mirror laid along the diagonal line $y = x$.

The reason for this will become clear upon reflection. Changing the coordinates from (2,5) to (5,2) flips a point across the diagonal line.

Inverse functions can really be useful in solving problems. It's not critical to understand exactly why or how now--we will see more on this later. But one quick example might give you an idea of what's going on:

Here are the graphs of two functions:

$$f(x) = 2x + 4$$

$$g(x) = \frac{1}{2}x - 2$$

Notice that these graphs are mirror images of each other; that is, each graph is the inverse of the other.

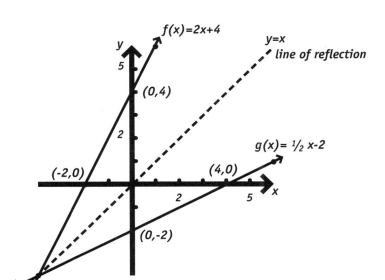

Now, check this out. Plug $x = 3$ into f and compute the answer, then plug that answer into g.

$$f(3) = (2)(3) + 4$$

$$= 6 + 4$$

$$= 10.$$

Plugging 10 into g, we get

$$g(10) = \left(\frac{1}{2}\right)(10) - 2$$

$$= 5 - 2$$

$$= 3.$$

You get back to your starting point, 3.

Let's try another one. If you plug $x = 2$ into $f(x)$

$$f(2) = (2)(2) + 4$$

$$= 4 + 4$$

$$= 8.$$

Then, plugging 8 into g, you end up with 2 again:

$$g(8) = \left(\frac{1}{2}\right)(8) - 2$$

$$= 4 - 2$$

$$= 2.$$

The same thing happens for any starting point. The functions f and g counteract each other. If you apply f to a number, you can reverse that operation by applying g to the result. This is the reason that f and g are inverses of each other.

Just as addition is considered the inverse of subtraction, and division is the inverse of multiplication, g is the inverse of f. It has the opposite, antidote effect—it undoes the effect of f. So you can think of g as the antidote to f.

This is pretty much how inverse functions work: If $f(x)$ tells you the number of bullwhips after a certain number of days, x, then $g(x)$ will tell you the number of days it will take for Simon to have x number of bullwhips. Earlier we used a function to compute the number of bullwhips for a given number of days. The inverse function will solve the opposite problem: it will compute the number of days for a given number of bullwhips.

Standard Deviant Hot Tip

Graphs aside, there is also a technique that works directly on the equation of a function to turn it into its inverse.

- ⊙ The equation is $f(x) = 2x + 4$.

- ⊙ Just swap the x and the $f(x)$, and change f to g.

- ⊙ This gives you $x = 2g(x) + 4$.

- ⊙ We use $g(x)$ to distinguish this inverse function from the first one, $f(x)$.

In terms of the whipmeister, the function we saw before, $f(x)$, allows you to compute how many whips Simon will stock on a given day. The inverse function, $g(x)$, would allow you to figure the day on which Simon would have a given number of whips. Generally, inverse functions are important any time you want to reverse your sense of which variable is supposed to be given, and which variable is to be computed. Cool, yah?

One word of caution–when you invert a graph, you don't always get a function. Consider this example:

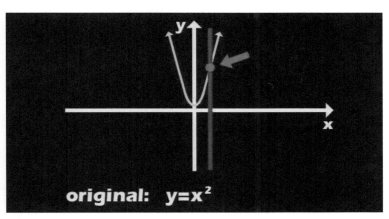

original: y=x²

We can use the vertical line test to be sure that this is a function. Sure enough, the vertical line never touches the graph at more than one point.

`0:39:54`

Now look at what happens when we invert the graph.

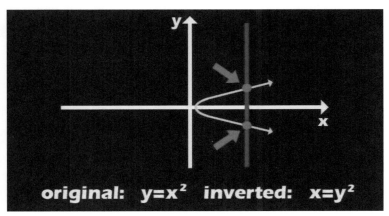

original: y=x² inverted: x=y²

41

STUDY SIDEKICK

The inverted graph fails the vertical line test.

This is a case where inverting the original function does not produce another function. This problem relates back to the idea that the result of the function must be exactly one value.

If we tell you x is 2, you can use the original graph to figure out what y has to be, and then there is just one answer.

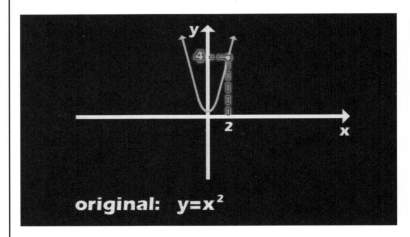

original: $y = x^2$

But the process is not reversible. If we say y is 4, there are two possible x values: either $x = 2$ or $x = -2$.

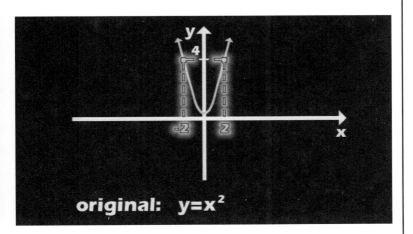

original: $y=x^2$

There is no way to choose one over the other. This shows that x is not expressible as a function of y, and explains why the inverted graph fails the vertical line test.

Okay, that's it for inverse functions for now. Don't stress about them—just know that they exist. And we'll be learning plenty about them later on.

Quiz 2

1. The domain of a function is the set of all values used by the _____ variable (which is often called x).

2. The range of a function is the set of all values used by the _____ variable (which is often called $f(x)$ or y).

3. A function may pair an element of its domain with _____ element(s) of its range.

4. A function may pair an element of its range with _____ element(s) of its domain.

5. The horizontal axis of a graph represents values for the _____ variable.

6. The range of a function is graphed on the _____ axis of a graph.

7. If an equation is graphed and the vertical line test shows that the graph of the equation is touched by the line _____ time(s), no matter where you apply the test, the equation is a function.

Quiz

8. Inverting a graph means that you _____ the coordinates for each point on the graph, so the points (0, 3), (2, 26), and (−0.002, 13) would become _____, _____, and _____.

9. What is the inverse function of $f(x) = 6x + 10$?

10. What is the inverse function of $f(x) = \dfrac{3x}{2} - \dfrac{2}{5}$?

`0:41:08`

`0:41:13`

Linear Equations

Section A: Algebraic Properties

If the function is the basic building block for algebra, the tools we use to manipulate these building blocks are called **algebraic properties**. There are six basic algebraic properties we can use to change the form of a function or an equation.

Remember, for all of these properties, we are talking about **real numbers**. Imaginary numbers are trickier, but we'll get to them later.

Just remember that a real number is any number that can be represented as a decimal. This decimal can be finite, such as $\frac{3}{2}$ or 1.5. It can also be repeating, such as $\frac{2}{3}$ or 0.666666... Or it can be infinite *without* repeating, such as pi, 3.14159265359... All of these are real numbers.

Each of the six properties we're about to discuss can be used to manipulate equations to make them easier to deal with. Let's say, for example, that you have an equation in the form

$$3y - 6x = 3$$

The equation $3y - 6x = 3$ is *not* in **standard form** for a function because neither variable is alone on one side of the equation. As we said, one thing you have to do over and over again in algebra is put an equation into some standard form. To do this, you use algebraic properties. In this example, we will isolate y on one side. Then y will be expressed as a function of x in the standard form.

How do we isolate the y value? First we can add $6x$ to *both* sides of the equation.

$$3y - 6x = 3$$

$$3y - 6x + (6x) = 3 + (6x)$$

We can do this because when two things are equal, like the two sides of an equation, adding the same quantity to each side will produce equal results. So the first step is logically acceptable.

0:42:35

RANDOM TRIVIA:

What piece of magical jewelry did "Burger King" possess?

On which body part could you find this piece of magic jewelry?

Read ahead for the answers

But why do we do it? The answer goes back to the idea of inverse operations.

Let's go back to our equation. On the left side we have

$$3y - 6x.$$

Originally, we had $3y$ but then $6x$ was subtracted from it. We want to undo that subtraction and get back to $3y$, which is closer to an isolated y. The opposite of subtracting $6x$ is adding $6x$. That's why we add $6x$ to the left of the equation, and of course we must also add it to the right to keep the two sides equal. Now we have

$$3y - 6x + (6x) = 3 + (6x).$$

The left side gets simplified to just $3y$.

Our equation is now

$$3y = 3 + 6x$$

So far, so good. The y is almost isolated. But we want y alone, and we have $3y$. That's three times too big. We want just one-third of that amount.

Remember,
whatever you
do to the right
side of the
equation, you
have to do
to the left
side of the
equation also.

So, multiply the left side by $\frac{1}{3}$. Of course, you must also multiply the right side by $\frac{1}{3}$ to keep the two sides equal.

The result is

$$\frac{1}{3} \text{ times } 3y = \frac{1}{3} \text{ times } (3 + 6x)$$

That simplifies to

$$y = \frac{1}{3}(3 + 6x)$$

At this point y is isolated, but the right side of the equation can still be simplified a little:

$$= \frac{1}{3}(3 + 6x)$$

$$= \frac{1}{3}(3) + \left(\frac{1}{3}\right)(6x)$$

$$= 1 + 2x$$

So, the final equation is

$$y = 1 + 2x.$$

We see in this form that y is a function of x, so we can put the equation into standard form: $f(x) = 1 + 2x$.

In each step of the last example, we made use of commonly understood properties of numbers. For example, the idea that one-third of the total of two numbers is the same as taking one-third of each and then adding. These properties have been given names:

Identity	(for addition or multiplication)
Commutative	(for addition or multiplication)
Associative	(for addition or multiplication)

Inverse (for addition or multiplication)

Closure (for addition or multiplication)

Distributive (for addition and multiplication)

Most of these operations and properties are based on common sense, and some may look so familiar to you that they are second nature. You might not even know that they had names for some of this stuff. But check it out, some folks are downright obsessive about the names of things, so it might be important for you to know which name goes with which property, or even to know what the full list of properties is. This definitely depends on your particular algebra class.

All right, here we go. Let's go through the property listings.

0:47:48

The **additive identity property** means that adding 0 to any number leaves that number unchanged. So:

$$3 + 0 = 3.$$

More formally:

$$x + 0 = x.$$

The **multiplicative identity property** means that multiplying any number times 1 leaves that number unchanged. So:

$$3(1) = 3$$

More formally:

$$1(x) = x.$$

The **commutative addition property** means that the order of addition doesn't matter, so:

$$3 + 4 = 4 + 3.$$

More abstractly, we say:

$$x + y = y + x.$$

The **inexpensive property** says that land purchased between a rat-infested abandoned building and a leaking sewage treatment plant is inexpensive property.

More abstractly, we say that

$$x = \text{property sold}$$

$$x = \text{cheap land}$$

The **commutative multiplication property** means that the order of multiplication doesn't matter, so:

$$(4)(7) = (7)(4)$$

More formally:

$$xy = yx,$$

STUDY SIDEKICK

`0:48:48`

The **associative property for addition** says that grouping in addition doesn't matter. In other words:

$$3 + (4 + 5) = (3 + 4) + 5.$$

They both equal 12. Okay? Remember, associative law—think free association—groups don't matter and are nonbinding.

Once again becoming abstract, the associative property for addition is written as:

$$x + (y + z) = (x + y) + z$$

where x, y, and z are all real numbers.

Standard Deviant Hot Tip

Recall that, when faced with an expression in parentheses, you are supposed to evaluate the parts inside the parentheses first, then do the other indicated operations.

I'm ugly, ugly, ugly.

-Jan Brady

The **associative multiplication property** says that grouping in multiplication doesn't matter either. So:

$$3(4 \cdot 5) = (3 \cdot 4)5$$

They both equal 60. Once again, associative equals free association.

So, we write this property more formally as:

$$x\,(yz) = (xy)\,z$$

with x, y, and z all being real numbers.

Standard Deviant Hot Tip

Recall that, although multiplication is often indicated by a dot between the factors to be multiplied together, often the dot is left out. When you don't see a specific sign that tells you what operation is to be done, it will be multiplication.

The **additive inverse property** says that every number has an opposite, and opposites add to 0. So:

The opposite of 3 is –3 and $3 + (-3) = 0$.

In other words, $x + (-x) = 0$, where x and $-x$ are each the additive inverse of the other.

The **multiplicative inverse property** means that every number except 0 has a reciprocal, and reciprocals multiply to give 1. So:

The reciprocal of 3 is $\frac{1}{3}$ and 3 times $\frac{1}{3}$ is 1.

Written more formally, we would say that for every x except 0, there is a number $\frac{1}{x}$, that, when multiplied by x, produces the answer 1, or $x\left(\frac{1}{x}\right) = 1$.

0:49:25

The **closure property** simply means that addition and multiplication are defined for any two numbers. That is, you can always add, subtract, or multiply any two numbers, even though you may not be able to divide them. For instance, you cannot divide anything by 0. It won't work.

Thought of another way, the closure property means that you will always get a real number as an answer if you start with real numbers. There is no way you could get a gold bracelet as an answer, nice as that might be.

Note that **closure** also refers to the proper and responsible way to end a relationship. For example, cheating on your loved one, waiting a week, and then returning to admit that you cheated on him/her with his/her best friend, and then formally breaking up is an example of **closure**.

0:49:50

Finally, the **distributive property** says that if you multiply the sum of two numbers by a third number, that's the same as multiplying each by the third number and then adding. So:

$$3(2 + 4) = (3 \cdot 2) + (3 \cdot 4).$$

More formally:

$$x\,(y + z) = xy + xz$$

All right, this one is key. The distributive property is probably the most important one for algebra, because it justifies the simplification of polynomials like $3x + 4x$, letting you manipulate them to your specific needs. After all, $3x + 4x$ really means

$$(3 \cdot x) + (4 \cdot x) = (3+4)x.$$

This type of factoring is crucial for you to know, as you will see. The distributive property is also critical in simplifying complicated multiplications of polynomials. We will see this later in connection with something called FOIL. That's where the distributive property really SHINES.

As a further review of these properties, let's look at the ones we used in our earlier example. Here is a step-by-step replay, in slow motion.

Here is $3y - 6x = 3$, our starting equation:

$$3y - 6x = 3$$

The next step uses additive inverses, or the fact that $6x$ is the opposite of $-6x$. Also through closure, we know that adding is possible, no matter what number x is.

$$(3y - 6x) + 6x = 3 + 6x$$

Then, through the associative property for addition, we grouped the $-6x$ and the $6x$ together to be added, even though in the original equation $3y$ and $-6x$ were grouped together.

$$3y + (-6x + 6x) = 3 + 6x$$

The additive identity said $3y$ plus 0 is still $3y$.

$$3y + (0) = 3 + 6x$$

$$3y = 3 + 6x$$

Then multiplicative inverses used the fact that $\frac{1}{3}$ is the reciprocal of 3. And again, through closure we know that multiplying is possible no matter what x's value is.

$$\left(\frac{1}{3}\right)(3y) = \left(\frac{1}{3}\right)(3 + 6x)$$

The associative property for multiplication allowed us to group the $\frac{1}{3}$ and the 3, to be multiplied, even though the 3 was originally grouped with y.

$$(1)y = \left(\frac{1}{3}\right)(3 + 6x)$$

The multiplicative identity says any number times 1 is itself.

$$(1)y = \left(\frac{1}{3}\right)(3 + 6x)$$

$$y = \left(\frac{1}{3}\right)(3 + 6x)$$

And finally, the distributive property let us multiply $\frac{1}{3}$ by 3 and $\frac{1}{3}$ by $6x$ separately, to give us $1 + 2x$.

$$y = \left(\frac{1}{3} \cdot 3\right) + \left(\frac{1}{3} \cdot 6x\right)$$

$$y = 1 + 2x.$$

You can see why some of these properties are important if we consider some situations in which similar properties do NOT hold. Like, closure seems pretty pointless, so you can add or multiply by anything, so what? But closure doesn't hold for division! It is not always possible to divide two numbers because you can never divide by 0.

RANDOM TRIVIA:

How did "Burger King" activate the powers of his magical ring?

Read ahead for the answer.

In the equation

$$xy = 3x$$

you might want to isolate y by dividing both sides by x:

$$\frac{xy}{x} = \frac{3x}{x}$$

That is fine, as long as x is not 0. But of course, x is a variable. You don't know what x is. So your little plan might be okay, or it might be a mistake, depending on the value of x. You just don't know.

But adding something to both sides of an equation never leads to that kind of problem, because addition is always going to work out fine. You've got closure to thank for that. Closure under addition says, "Don't worry—add to both sides and be happy."

And while we're complaining about division, we can notice that the associative property doesn't apply to division, either. Yes, division bites.

Consider

$$18/6/3$$

Does that mean divide 18 by 6 to get 3, then divide that by 3 to get 1? Or does it mean divide 6 by 3 to get 2, and then divide 18 by 2 to get 9? The answers are different, *so grouping does matter in division.*

Grouping can lead to errors in using a calculator. How would you do $\frac{1}{4}$ divided by $\frac{1}{8}$ on your calculator? If you enter 1 divided by 4 divided by 1 divided by 8, you will get the wrong answer. This is because the calculator assumes you want to group things from left to right. But the problem really calls for this grouping:

$$\frac{\frac{1}{4}}{\frac{1}{8}}$$

You can put things in parentheses on most calculators, but it is annoying that you have to remember to do that. Life is much simpler when you are multiplying or adding.

Video Notes

Section B: Linear Equations and Slope

Now remember, all functions are basically graphs. The simplest form that a function can take is a linear equation; that is, a function with a graph that's a straight line. A linear relation has a constant rate of decrease or a constant rate of increase, like our whipmeister, Simon, whose bullwhips increased at a constant rate of 2 per day. Later, you will see how this is different from a quadratic equation, where the rate of increase or decrease changes so the graph of the function is not straight. We'll save those bad boys for later—but meanwhile let's look at two examples of linear equations.

⊙ Sue is charged $3 to be connected to the "Psychic Specialists" 1-900 line. She is also charged $1 for each minute she is on the line. Sue's total charge, y, as a function of the number of minutes on the line, x, is given by

$$y = x + 3.$$

⊙ Now take paranoid Dave, who has $500,000 under his mattress. He spends it at a rate of $25,000 per year. Dave's fortune, y, as a function of the number of years he has been spending it, x, is given by

$$y = -25,000x + 500,000.$$

Notice that each of these functions is a linear equation that can be graphed, and both look a little like our earlier example of Simon.

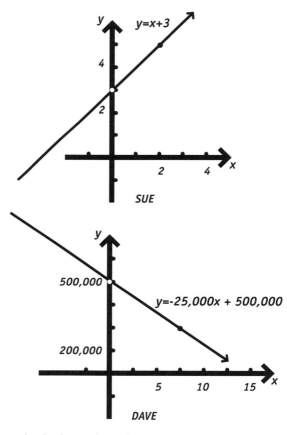

Before we even think about these function examples in depth, we need to recognize another standard form:

0:57:06

the slope-intercept form of a linear equation:

$$y = mx + b$$

60

> Any linear relation of a constant increase or decrease,
> like our examples, can be represented by an equation
> in the form:
>
> $$y = mx + b.$$
>
> This very important equation is the key to graphing
> linear equations.

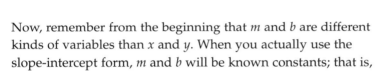

Now, remember from the beginning that m and b are different
kinds of variables than x and y. When you actually use the
slope-intercept form, m and b will be known constants; that is,
they will have a fixed value within each equation.

For example, in Sue's equation $y = x + 3$, the value of m is 1
and the value of b is 3. For Dave's money, m equals –25,000 and
b equals 500,000. In general, m is the coefficient of x and b is the
constant term (with no x).

In a slope-intercept form equation, y takes the place of $f(x)$.
Remember, **y and $f(x)$ are interchangeable** so it doesn't matter
too much which one you write—it's just the way you write it.
So **m will be the slope of the line**. And **b is the y-intercept**, or
the point on the vertical y-axis that the graph will go through.

`0:59:50`

Bottom line: The **slope** of a line is the rate of change between
two points. The easiest way to think of slope is as a ratio of rise
over run.

⊙ **Run** is horizontal change, or change along the x-axis in a
horizontal direction. That is, right or left from one point on
the line to another. *Change to the left is negative; change to the
right is positive.*

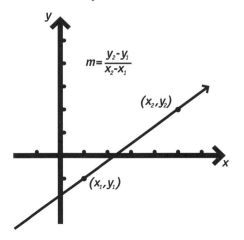

"Rise over Run"

◉ **Rise** is vertical change, or change along the y-axis in a vertical direction. That is, up or down, from one point on the line to another. Vertically, up is positive, down is negative. So slope is the ratio of y change to x change: the rise divided by the run. There's an easy formula for finding the slope of a line that looks like you see here:

$$m = \frac{y_2 - y_1}{x_2 - x_1}$$

(x_2, y_2)

(x_1, y_1)

(x_1, y_1) and (x_2, y_2) are two points that you know on the line. $y_2 - y_1$ is the change in y, or rise, and $x_2 - x_1$, is the change in x or the run.

Given any two points on a line, you can come up with the slope of that line. For example, let's say we know that the points $(-1, -1)$ and $(2, 5)$ are on a particular line, and we want to find the slope of that line. Note that these are two of the ordered pairs we came up with earlier when we talked about domain and range.

In this example the change in the "rise," or y values, is

$$5 - (-1) = 6.$$

The change in the x values, or "run," is

$$x_2 - x_1 \text{ or } 2 - (-1) = 3.$$

So $x=3$.

The "rise over run" is $= \frac{6}{3}$ or 2.

So our slope is 2.

STUDY SIDEKICK

Standard Deviant Hot Tip

Here's a trick to remember how to find slopes. In our example to get from point $(-1,-1)$ to point $(2,5)$, we went up 6 and over 3.

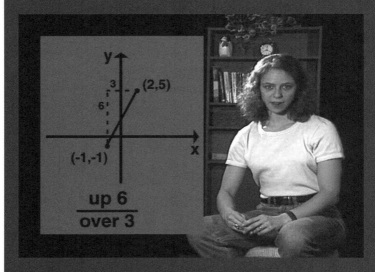

That is, UP 6, OVER 3. So the slope is up 6 divided by 3, or "up 6, over 3," or 2.

It is important to make sure that you compare the change in y and the change in x in the correct order. Just make sure to subtract the correct points from each other. In other words, be sure to subtract point 1 from point 2, or vice versa, for both x and y values.

If you mix them up, then your result will have a sign error, your slope will be wrong, you'll fail college algebra and face punishment, ridicule, and possibly execution. *Don't* let this happen to you!

The magic of our formula $y = mx + b$ is that given two points on a line, you can determine the equation that describes the whole line. First you find the slope, then you find the y-intercept, then you plug your numbers into the standard form.

So you know how to get the slope, but you still need the y-intercept. Once you have the slope, it's easy to find the y-axis intercept, or b value. Our equation is in the form:

$$y = mx + b$$

and we want to determine b, so we must isolate b by subtracting mx from both sides:

$$y - mx = mx + b - mx$$

This leaves us with:

$$y - mx = b.$$

Since we already know values for x, y, and m, we just plug 'em in and calculate the value of b.

Going back to our example, we found the slope, m, to be 2. We know one point on the line is (2, 5), so:

$$x = 2 \ and \ y = 5.$$

Plugging these numbers in we get:

$$y - mx = b$$

$$5 - (2 \cdot 2) = b$$

$$5 - 4 = b$$

$$1 = b$$

So

$$1 = b.$$

If the chickens had a revolution, it would be really confusing, since we'd have to say, "There's a coup in the coop!" That's pretty hard to say.

-Matt May

We can now put our equation together knowing the slope m and y intercept b, and we finally get

$$y = 2x + 1.$$

H   U   R   R   A   Y   Y   Y   !   !   !

We've just found an equation for a line in slope-intercept form using only two points on the line. But there's more than one way to do a problem in algebra. You have mastered the slope-intercept form but what about the point-slope formula of a linear equation?

1:04:00

⊙   With the **point-slope formula**, you can find the equation of a line with just two points as your starting information.

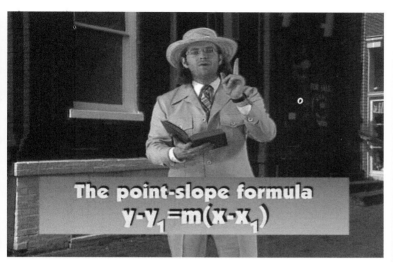

The point-slope formula
$y - y_1 = m(x - x_1)$

The general equation looks like this:

$$y - y_1 = m (x - x_1)$$

1:05:54

Let's find the equation of a line in standard form with only two points: (3, 12) and (1, 2).

First, find the slope:

$$\text{slope} = \frac{\text{rise}}{\text{run}}$$

so: $\dfrac{12 - 2}{3 - 1}$

$$= \frac{10}{2}$$

slope = 5

Next, plug 5 into the point-slope formula for *m*, and then plug one of the ordered pairs into the formula. We'll use (1,2). You get

$$y - y_1 = m(x - x_1)$$

$$y - 2 = 5(x - 1).$$

Now, use the algebraic properties you know to switch stuff around. First multiply 5 times the quantity $(x - 1)$ to get $5x - 5$:

$$y - 2 = 5x - 5$$

Then isolate the *y* by adding 2 to both sides of the equation. You get:

$$y = 5x - 3.$$

Guess what, that's the standard equation for the line. Ain't the point-slope formula easy?

Okay, using all of our new-found algebra knowledge about slope and *y*-intercept, let's look at our earlier examples in detail.

We said that Sue pays $3 to be connected to the "Psychic Specialists" 1-900 line. She is then charged $1 for each minute she's on the line. This is a linear relation between the amount of time Sue spends on the "Psychic Specialists" 1-900 line in minutes, and how much it costs her. Let's graph the line of Sue's equation.

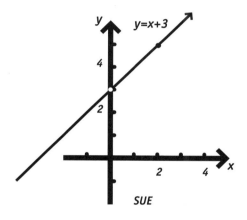

On the graph, the x-axis represents time, or the number of minutes Sue is on the phone. The y-axis represents money—how much Sue's racked up in a phone bill.

At time $x = 0$, Sue has already been charged $3 for a connection fee, so the y-axis intercept is 3. That is, the graph shows how Sue already owes $3 at 0 minutes.

After 1 minute, and for each minute afterward, Sue pays 1 additional dollar. That means the rate of change, or slope, is 1 dollar per minute.

Sue's equation is y equals $1x + 3$, or, simply, $y = x + 3$. Plugging in any value of time for x, we can find the amount of money that Sue has been charged up to that time.

For example, if she spends 10 minutes talking to her favorite psychic, we plug in 10 for x (time):

$$x = 10$$

So
$$y = 10 + 3 = 13$$

After 10 minutes Sue has spent $13.

If Sue spends 2 hours on the "Psychic Specialists" line, then:

$$x = 120$$

So
$$y = 120 + 3 = 123.$$

After 2 hours Sue has spent $123.

Notice that, once we have the graph of the line that fits Sue's situation, she can also plan for her future calls by checking how much time she gets for how much money she wants to spend. So, after this graph has been accurately drawn, Sue won't need to solve the equation again (well, not until the rates change); she can just look at the graph.

Note further that for both Sue and whipmeister Simon, the constant change is an increase, so the slope is positive and the graph rises from left to right. Now let us turn our attention to Dave, the man with his money under his mattress.

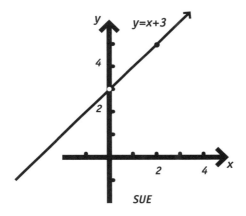

SUE

Dave has $500,000 under his mattress. He spends it at a rate of $25,000 per year. This is another relation between time and money, with time now measured in years instead of minutes.

However, we are now dealing with an initial condition of having $500,000, and a constant decrease from this initial condition.

At the beginning Dave has $500,000, so:

$$y = 500,000$$

71

After 1 year Dave has $500,000 minus the amount of money he spent this year:

$$\$500{,}000 - \$25{,}000 = \$475{,}000$$

After another year Dave has $475,000 minus the amount of money he spent over that year, $25,000.

Dave's function is

$$y = -25{,}000x + 500{,}000.$$

The important concept to see here is that for Dave, as opposed to Sue and Simon, the constant change is a decrease, so the slope is negative and the graph falls from left to right. To go from point (0, 500,000) to point (1, 475,000), you go down 25,000 and over 1. That's a slope of –25,000.

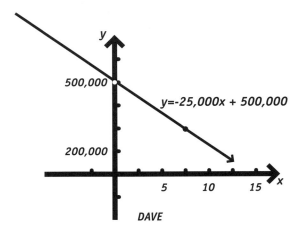

In each of our examples, y changes from an initial position (or state) at a constant rate, relative to x.

For Sue, the change as her bill rises is a constant increase, but the dip in Dave's stash is a constant decrease. Therefore, both of these situations can be modeled by a linear equation.

STUDY SIDEKICK

Section C: Properties of Linear Graphs

Just by observing the graph of a linear equation, it is possible to learn some things about it. It should already be apparent that changing the value of b will change where the graph of the equation crosses the y-axis.

If b equals 0, the line will cross the y-axis at the origin, point (0, 0). If b equals 3, the line will cross the y-axis at (0, 3), and so on.

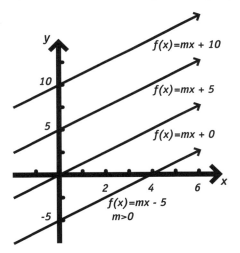

The slope, or value of m, also affects the graph of a linear equation. Changes in the value of m will change the gradient, or steepness, of the line.

If the slope $m = 0$, the graph of the equation will be a horizontal line, since a slope of 0 indicates a rise of 0 (no vertical movement over a run of any distance). As m increases from 0, the slope increases, or gets steeper, from left to right. The larger the slope, the steeper the gradient of the line.

Look at this graph with a slope (a rise) of 100
over a run of 1.

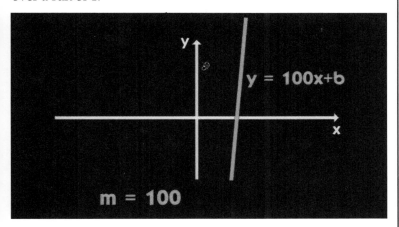

It is nearly vertical already. A line with slope 1,000 would be
steeper still. And as the line becomes closer to vertical, the slope
gets larger and larger as it approaches infinity, which is the
slope of a vertical line.

1:13:31

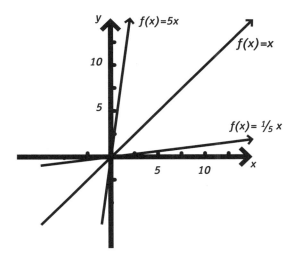

75

Infinity, like imaginary numbers and several other concepts you will encounter during your study of algebra, is an abstract concept. That is, it can be difficult to grasp, because it does not, technically, exist on planet Earth. Yet it is a useful mathematical concept anyway. To become comfortable with such ideas you must, as they say, suspend your disbelief…like when you were a kid and you actually believed that Santa, the Easter Bunny, and Hank the Hanukkah Hippo really did exist.

The slope of a line can also be negative, which indicates that the line drops from left to right. As m decreases from 0, the graph slopes more and more downward from left to right, like in the following graph.

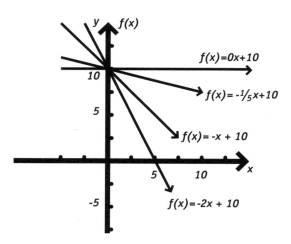

And of course, if you get a hold of one of those handy graphing calculators, you can explore on your own using different values for m and b and drawing your own conclusions about how the different variable values change the graph.

Two more easy things to remember about slopes:

First, lines with the same slope are parallel, like these, see?

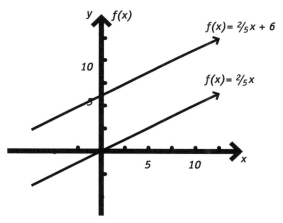

All have the same *m* value, or slope, and they are all parallel to each other.

Second, perpendicular lines have slopes that are each other's negative reciprocal—that is, if your lines have the slopes of

$$3 \text{ and } -\frac{1}{3}$$

then you know the lines are perpendicular to each other, no matter what their *y*-intercepts are.

And if you are given lines with slopes of:

$$-\frac{12}{5} \text{ and } \frac{5}{12}$$

You'd know that the lines are perpendicular:

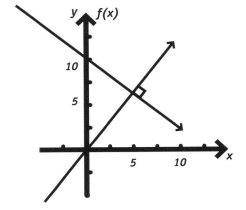

Section D: Roots

`1:16:41`

The last crucial concept we encounter with linear equations is the root of a function. We've been talking about the y-intercept: the place where the graph of a function crosses the y-axis. Well, the x-intercept, or any point where the graph of a function crosses the x-axis, is considered a **root of the function**.

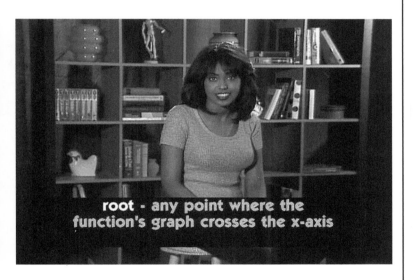

root - any point where the function's graph crosses the x-axis

`1:17:05`

Every linear function has a root—except those with 0 slopes, which are horizontal lines and run parallel to the x-axis forever. Remember that the x-axis itself is a horizontal line, and is the graph of the equation

$$y = 0.$$

I guess I shouldn't have eaten all those funny brownies.
- Salvador Dali

You can identify the root on a graph simply by looking at where the line crosses the x-axis, which is the point where y equals 0. Mathematically, this position can be found by setting y equal to 0 and solving the equation for x:

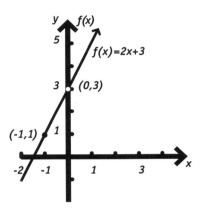

Given a specific function, say $f(x) = 2x + 3$, here is how to find the root, or x-intercept.

We know that the point at which we seek y, or $f(x)$, has a value of 0, so substituting 0 for $f(x)$ gives us:

$$0 = 2x + 3.$$

Now isolate x using the properties of algebra.

Subtract 3 from both sides to get

$$-3 = 2x$$

Then divide both sides by 2 to find that:

$$x = \frac{-3}{2}$$

So, for the function:

$$f(x) = 2x + 3$$

The root or x-intercept is:

$$\frac{-3}{2}.$$

These same steps can be performed with any other equation in the form $y = mx + b$. BUT there's a twist...you can also find the x-intercept with the formula:

1:18:51

$$x = \frac{-b}{m}$$

Note that in our example:

$$m = 2,$$

$$b = 3$$

the root or x-intercept is

$$\frac{-3}{2}, \text{ which happens to be } \frac{-b}{m}$$

> This is a general rule: the x-intercept, or root, of a linear equation can always be found by dividing the negative of the y intercept, $-b$, by the slope m. You may find the root by using this rule, or by following the steps we used earlier. But watch out...many professors want to see your steps, and will prefer to see you go through the algebra above, rather than just plugging the slope and y-intercept into the rule. In these cases, use the rule to check your work over quickly.

1:20:02

There are actually some practical applications for roots. Since the root is the value for x where $y = 0$, it can be useful to determine how long it will be in time before, say, Dave has run out of money, or until y (money) $= 0$.

We just gave you the formula for finding the x-axis intercept, or the point on the graph where $y = 0$. Remember? It was

$$x = \frac{-b}{m}$$

In Dave's case:

$$b = 500{,}000$$

$$m = -25{,}000$$

$$x = \frac{-500{,}000}{-25{,}000}$$

$$= 20.$$

After 20 years, Dave will have run out of money.

We will look for roots again and again in algebra, so you can always remember this key definition: A root of a function is any point where the function's graph crosses the x-axis, and it is also where $y = 0$.

A linear equation will always have only one root because a straight line can cross the x-axis only one time (but what about lines parallel to the x-axis?). But we'll find more roots as we explore more complicated, higher order polynomials.

> ### Standard Deviant Hot Tip
>
> Here's a trick. Want a handy way to know how many roots are in a polynomial equation? Just look at the degree of the equation. A first-degree equation—one with x to the first power, like a linear equation—has one root. Second-degree equations have two roots. Third-degrees equations—those with x^3 have three roots. And it works every time; the number of roots in a polynomial equation is as high as the degree.

But what about our horizontal line:

$$f(x) = y = 3?$$

It doesn't have a degree in it, does it? Actually when we rewrite the function as

$$f(x) = y = 3x^0 ,$$

then it does. Remember that $x^0 = 1$ for any x and, since the degree of x is 0, there are 0 roots to this equation. No roots in $y = 3$.

Doctor, doctor, doctor, doctor and doctor.

-Spies Like Us

And that pretty much covers slopes, graphs, and roots of linear equations. If you have any questions or some things still have you confused, just reread the workbook or watch the tape until all is clear.

Quiz 3

1. Match the algebraic property with the equation shown below:

A. _____ $x(yz) = (xy)z$

1. Additive identity property

B. _____ $x + y = y + x$

2. Associative property for addition

C. _____ $x(y + z) = xy + xz$

3. Commutative property for addition

D. _____ $x \cdot 1 = x$

4. Additive inverse property

E. _____ $xy = yx$

5. Distributive property

F. _____ $x + (-x) = 0$

6. Associative property for multiplication

G. _____ $x \cdot \dfrac{1}{x} = 1$

7. Commutative property for multiplication

H. _____ $x + 0 = x$

8. Multiplicative identity property

I. _____ $x + (y + z) = (x + y) + z$

9. Multiplicative inverse property

85

2. The slope of a line is the _____ of _____ between two points and is commonly thought of as the ratio of the _____ over the _____. Its symbol is ____.

3. Find the slope and *y*-intercept of the following equations:

   a. $y = .65x + 4$

   b. $f(x) = 3 - 2x$

4. Using the point-slope form, you can find the equation of a line with _____ point(s).

5. Find the equation of the line, given:

   a. $(-4, 0)$ and $(0, -2)$

   b. $(3, 6)$ and *y*-intercept $= 2$

6. Find the equation of a line parallel to $3x + y = 6$.

7. Find the slope of a line perpendicular to $3x + y = 6$.

8. A function's root is its _____ −intercept.

9. Find the root of $x + 2y = 14$.

10. The number of roots in a polynomial equation is equal to the _____ of the equation.

THE ANSWER MAN

The Answer Man is dedicated to alleviating the worries of his fellow Cerebellum employees. Each day, he receives hundreds of letters from coworkers. We have reprinted some of them here, with The Answer Man's responses. We hope they can be helpful to you, too.

Dear Answer Man,

Recently, everyone in the office got new computers. Meanwhile, I still work on an abacus. It's hard, day after day, moving those round beads from one side to the other. Everyone else has these newfangled "screen savers." And me? I have to shake my abacus up and down every two minutes for fear it will "freeze up." What's a poor office worker to do?

- Stone Aged

Dear Stone Aged:

After hours, go into another office in your company. Steal all the computer equipment you need, and install it at your desk. Make sure to write your name on the new computer with a black Magic Marker.

Dear Answer Man,

What is the best way to keep your eyebrows finely shaped and attractive?

- Wondering

Dear Wondering:

Who cares?

Dear Answer Man,

I have a Mr. Potato Head Massager on my desk and he's been making weird faces and gestures at me at odd times of the day... do you think it means he wants attention, or just needs a good skull to massage? I'm not sure what to do with him. Please help!

- Puzzled

Dear Puzzled:

Mr. Potato Head™ Massagers have psychic abilities, just like Electronic Talking Battleship™. Your head massager is obviously trying to warn you of impending danger. Heed his warnings!

Dear Answer Man,

About a month ago, I stole one of my coworker's computers and replaced it with an abacus. He doesn't seem to notice. I feel guilty about it, but he seems unstable. Should I tell him?

- Stickyfingers

Dear Stickyfingers:

Absolutely not. Don't ever let on that you stole his computer. If he should somehow replace his abacus with another computer, steal that one, too. Sit back and enjoy the hilarity as he feverishly tries to adjust. When you get a chance, steal his other possessions. Then, move one of your coworkers to a completely different office. When he inquires about where the co-worker went, insist that no one by that name has ever worked in your office. After a few weeks of this kind of treatment, he'll believe that reality is crumbling around him, and should burst out in tears every time someone says his name.

Answer Man

Dear Answer Man,

I have the following questions:

1. How many licks does it take to get to the center of a Tootsie Roll Pop?

2. What should I do if it burns when I urinate?

3. Where does the Answer Man get his answers?

4. What are the rules of using was/were? ie. "I wish I _____ going to get a new chair for my desk."

> \- Thanks,
>
> Questioning

Dear Questioning:

I have the following answers.

1. **That depends on how big your tongue is. The Answer Man takes 342 licks.**

2. **Stop drinking lighter fluid. Your symptoms will subside.**

3. **None of your business, jerk.**

4. **When in doubt, use were.**

Get a hobby.

Hey Answer Man:

I don't feel like doing my work today. How can I look busy without actually doing anything? Any suggestions?

> \- Lazy in McLean

Dear Lazy:

If I had a dollar for every way I know how to look busy, I'd have about eight dollars.

STUDY SIDEKICK

1. Keep your desk cluttered. The only people with messy desks are the ones who don't have time to clean. This will mask the fact that you aren't doing anything.

2. Whenever you have a chance to select your own projects, choose the project with the most prep time. All that legwork offers ample opportunities to leave the office and get distracted.

3. Read the material on your screen intently. Prop your head up with your hands. Your hands should obscure your face. Sleep.

4. Crawl under your desk. Pull in the chair. Sleep.

5. Call the time and temperature service. Listen for an hour or so. Whenever someone looks at you, wear a troubled expression and say things into the phone like: "Now you're wasting MY time!" and "Who told him he could do that?"

6. Look in the file cabinet. Shout: "I can't find a damned thing in here!" Rearrange the files, being careful to read each one thoroughly.

7. Think of as many reasons as you can to leave the office. Use them. Examples: "Who needs pens?!!" or "Better check on my car alarm!"

8. Eat your lunch at the office. Don't eat it all during your lunch hour. Continue working on it from time to time during the afternoon.

Dear Answer Man,

How long can I keep this up before I start to grow hair on the inside of my palms?

- Rosey Palmer

Dear Palmer,

Well, duh. Rogaine™ goes on your head, not your palms.

Dear Answer Man,

Why don't we concentrate on producing fusion as an energy source, as it is an unlimited source of clean energy?

– Pondering

Dear Pondering:

Even if we concentrate as hard as we can, the human body isn't capable of producing fusion. Where'd you learn physics?

Dear Answer Man,

Why does everybody wait to the last moment to get something done and call everyone else a procrastinator?

- Indignant

Dear Indignant:

I do everything at the last minute. I call everyone else procrastinators to divert attention from me. As long as everyone is concentrating on everyone else, I'm free to be irresponsible.

Dear Answer Man,

Why is it that men and women are meant to be together but have problems communicating?

- Heartbroken

Dear Heartbroken:

Men and women are meant simply to mate. There is no grand design for them to be together—that's why they can't communicate.

Dear Answer Man,

I have lived my life by the magic eight ball. It has brought me good times and bad, but recently it told me that my wife has been cheating on me. And when I asked it what I should do it said, "The answer is very cloudy." Does that mean I should return the shotgun and shells?

-Disgruntled

Dear Disgruntled:

SIGNS

POINT

TO YES

Dear Answer Man,

My boss loves disco. I love my boss. What should I do?

-Befuddled

Dear Befuddled:

The rules of logic are simple here. Sleep with disco.

PRACTICE EXAM 1

Graphing Problems

Using the graph paper on the next pages of the workbook, graph the following:

1. $y = 4x - 2$

2. $y + 1 = x + 3(x - 1)$

3. $6x - 24y = 36$

4. $2x = 8$

5. $y = 1$

Word Problems

6. A rectangular box has a length 3 times its width. If it's 4 inches wide, what is its perimeter (remember that the perimeter of a rectangle is the distance around it)?

7. A math student is 18 years old. If one cousin will be three times the student's age when the student is 25, how old is that cousin now? If a second cousin will be one-half the student's age in four more years, how old is the second cousin?

8. A hot drink machine in the student lounge can fill a paper cup that is guaranteed to burn your fingers with terrible coffee in 30 seconds and can fill the same size paper cup with fake cream in 75 seconds. (a) If the timers on the dispensers are both broken so that nothing stops the terrible coffee and fake cream, how long will it take to fill up the cup? (b) If, at the same time, the cup has a small hole (burned into it by the first drop of coffee) that will drain a full cup in 120 seconds, how long will it take to fill the cup?

9. Evaluate the following expressions:

    a. $5 - 3(4 - 6)$

    b. $-(5 - 4) - (-7 - 6)$

10. Name the algebraic property shown in the following equations:

    a. $10 (x + y) + 0 = 10 (x + y)$

    b. $3(x + 4) = 3x + 12$

    c. $x(y + 3) = (y + 3)x$

    d. $10 (x + y) + z = z + 10 (x + y)$

11. Simplify, using the algebraic properties:

  a. $3(4x + 2)$

  b. $6(x - 4) + 3(2x + 5)$

  c. $(y^2 + 35y - 15) + 2(x^2 - y^2 - 16y + 5)$

12. Evaluate each of the following functions at the value shown:

  a. $f(x) = 3x + 12; x = 1$

  b. $g(x) = 5(1 - 6x); x = 3$

  c. $p(y) = 6y + 2(-3 + y) - 4y; \ y = 2$

13. Solve the following linear equations:

  a. $3x - 4 - (2x + 6) = 3 - x - 7$

  b. $4(2y + 5) - 3(y - 6) = 18$

  c. $2x + 3x(1 + 3) + 4(x + 3) = 2$

PRACTICE EXAM 2

1. Simplify the following expressions:

  a. $3[(-2)(6) + 4(-5 + 3 - 7)]$

  b. $\dfrac{5^2 - 2}{[(-2)(-3)-3]}$

2. Name the algebraic property shown in the following equations:

  a. $p^2(1) = p^2$

  b. $4(3) = 12$

  c. $2(5y) = (2 \cdot 5)y$

  d. $(7 + y) + p^2 = 7 + (y + p^2)$

3. Evaluate each of the following functions at the value shown:

  a. $f(x) = 3(4x + 2); x = 5$

  b. $g(x) = 6(x - 4) + 3(2x + 5); x = 4$

  c. $f(x) = 2(x^2 - 16x + 5); x = 2$

4. Find the equation of the line having the following slopes and passing through the following points.

    a. $m = 2$, $(4,2)$

    b. $m = 0$, $(3,1)$

    c. $m = -1$, $(2,3)$

5. Using the graph paper that follows, graph each of the following:

    a. $2x + 3y = 4$

    b. $3x + y = 0$

    c. $y + 4 = 5$

    d. $x + 3 = 2$

Heard any good jokes lately?

-Pee Wee Herman at the MTV Music Awards

STUDY SIDEKICK

VIDEO TIME CODE

The Adventurous World of College Algebra Part 2

98

VIDEO NOTES

0:02:57

The Adventurous World of College Algebra Part 2

Introduction to Quadratic Equations

All right. You know your algebra: functions, graphs, linear equations, point-slope, and slope-intercept forms, and... so it's not quite as exciting as bowling. However, as you journey

further into college algebra, you'll discover that although the formulas may change and the variables may get more complex, there's always one constant—adventure.

In the section, we will square your algebra knowledge with quadratic equations, roots, complex numbers, polynomials, and the different operations you can perform with all these mathematical marvels.

Here we go. The degree of a polynomial is the highest exponent that appears in the polynomial. A quadratic polynomial has a degree of 2.

For example:

$$x^2 \qquad\qquad 5x^2 - 2x + 3 \qquad\qquad 7 - x^2$$

So why do they call it quadratic? Doesn't that mean 4? In this instance, QUAD comes from the same root as the word QUADrilateral, which is a four-sided figure, like a square. An x with an exponent of 2 is called "x squared." QUADratic refers to the presence of a squared variable.

Interesting Aside:

Think about it this way: if you're an ancient Greek, you don't really have lots of paper and pencils or nifty calculators to use while you're figuring out mathematics. So what do you do? Some ancient Greeks used wet sand and made marks in the sand with specialized tools like branches. In those days, numbers were written as marks, and if you wanted to multiply them, you lined them up in a row and column with one mark common to both lines. Then you filled in the rest of the rows and columns and added up all the marks you just made (aren't calculators a REAL improvement?).

Continued on next page

For example, if you lined up three marks in a row and three marks in a column [the old way of writing (3)(3)], it would look like this:

Let's multiply by filling in the rows and columns.

Behold:

We have (3)(3) = 9 and 9 was a square number to the ancient Greeks. Literally. That's where the name came from.

Now back to the tape...

In linear equations, the only power of x that appears is the first power, $x^1 = x$. So linear equations have only first-degree polynomials. When you multiply two linear polynomials together, the result is always a quadratic equation. Before we chart a course into unknown quadratic regions on our search for x, let's briefly go over two items:

⊙ Squares and square root notation

⊙ Binomial multiplication

0:05:19

Section A: Squares and Square Root Notation

Remember: A number squared is simply that number multiplied by itself.

- ⊙ Two squared (2^2), or two times two $(2)(2)$, is 4.

- ⊙ Nine squared (9^2) is 9 times 9, or 81.

The square root operation is the inverse of squaring.

I drank what?

- Socrates

- ⊙ If we square 9, we get 81. Taking the square root of 81 reverses the process and gives you back 9.

- ⊙ If you square 1.2, you get 1.44. Reversing the process, the square root of 1.44 gives you back 1.2.

What is the square root of 25? You have to imagine the squaring operation and work backward: figure out what number squared results in 25.

$$5^2 = 25$$

The square root of any number a is the thing you multiply by itself to produce a.

For a few lucky examples, like 25 and 81, you can figure out the square root just by thinking about the problem. But unless your number is a perfect square, like 25 or 81, the most practical way to find a square root for most numbers will usually be with a calculator.

I give you
the calculator!

- The Standard
Deviants

Standard Deviant Hot Tip

When looking for the square root of a number you may get up to two answers: one positive and one negative. A calculator is designed to give just one of the two possible answers. It will always give the positive answer, and that one is called THE square root. So when we talk about THE square root of a number the answer is never negative.

There are two ways to indicate a square root of number. Both of them mean THE square root, the one that is positive:

1. **A radical sign**: $\sqrt{}$

Another radical sign:

MORE GOATS FOR PUBLIC OFFICE

2. **A fractional exponent**: $a^{1/2}$

Both are valid ways to write the quantity "the square root of "a."

Now let's look at the square root of 9:

$$\sqrt{9} \text{ or } 9^{1/2}$$

We know that 3 times itself equals 9, so 3 is the square root of 9. But -3 times -3 also equals 9. So the square root of 9 could be positive or negative 3.

> **When looking for a square root of a number, you may get two answers: one positive and one negative. We indicate this with:**
> $$\pm\sqrt{a}$$

When we talk about THE square root of a number, the answer is never negative. But there's this problem of two square roots of 9 (3 and -3). The same holds true for any number. Both 4 and -4 are square roots of 16, because squaring 4 gives 16 and squaring -4 also gives 16.

Remember, the radical symbol always refers to the positive square root. You must use a negative sign in front of the radical to indicate the negative square root. And if you see a plus-or-minus sign, that means that both positive and negative square roots are in play.

> *Standard Deviant Hot Tip*
>
> Nobody but your professor or Stephen Hawkings actually knows how to find a square root in his head, so like we said before, the best way to find the square root for most numbers is to use a calculator.

But it's a really good idea to know the simple ones by heart. What makes a square root simple? The square root of 16 is simple because 16 is a perfect square of the whole number 4. 4 times 4 is 16, so the square root of 16 is 4. Then, 5 times 5 is 25, so 25 is also a perfect square with a square root of 5. You get the idea.

Know These!

`0:10:58`

There are only 11 perfect squares from 0 to 100 and they all have simple roots:

$$0^2 = 0 \quad 1^2 = 1 \quad 2^2 = 4 \quad 3^2 = 9 \quad 4^2 = 16 \quad 5^2 = 25$$

$$6^2 = 36 \quad 7^2 = 49 \quad 8^2 = 64 \quad 9^2 = 81 \quad 10^2 = 100$$

They're pretty easy and it's important to be able to recognize them. It'll save you a lot of anguish in the long run. Imagine: any time you see $\sqrt{49}$ you'll know immediately to simplify it to 7. Whole numbers are a lot easier to work with than radicals.

SO LEARN YOUR SQUARE ROOTS! YOU WILL NEVER BE SORRY!

And in case you were wondering about square roots of negative numbers, wonder on, folks. We'll get there soon enough.

Section B: Multiplying Binomials

`0:12:00`

Just as a bicycle has two wheels and a biathlete has two sports, a binomial has two terms.

For example, linear polynomials like

$$7x - 4 \text{ and } 2x + 3$$

are all binomials. Monomial, binomial, and trinomial are all more specific versions of the term **polynomial**.

A linear polynomial is an expression with a degree of 1.

The Fabulous FOIL Method!

When multiplying two binomial expressions together we use a method called FOIL. FOIL is a handy combination of the commutative and distributive properties of algebra. FOIL stands for

"First, Outside, Inside, Last." This is the way you want to multiply out the terms of two binomials.

Here's an example with the binomial:

$$(2x + 1)^2 \text{ or } (2x + 1)(2x + 1)$$

To find the product of:

$$(2x+1)^2$$

1. Write the expression in the longhand form:

$$(2x+1)(2x+1)$$

2. Use FOIL. Multiply the two first terms, then the outside terms, then the inside terms, then the last terms.

3. This gives us:

$$(2x+1)(2x+1) =$$

$$4x^2 + 2x + 2x + 1$$

The **first terms** in the parentheses $(2x)(2x) = 4x^2$

The **outside terms** $(2x)(1) = 2x$

The **inside terms** $(1)(2x) = 2x$

The **last terms** $(1)(1) = 1$

4. Simplifying this, we get

$$4x^2 + 4x + 1$$

This FOIL method for multiplying binomial expressions can be used for any two binomials and can be modified to help find the product of higher order polynomials.

For instance, let's try the quantity:

$$(3x + 4)(x^3 - 2x^2)$$

Use FOIL:

F: $(3x)(x^3) = 3x^4$

O: $(3x)(-2x^2) = -6x^3$

I: $(4)(x^3) = 4x^3$

L: $(4)(-2x^2) = -8x^2$

Simplify:

$$3x^4 - 2x^3 - 8x^2$$

FOIL works for any two binomials. All that matters is that each pair of parentheses contains just two terms—it doesn't matter what form those terms take.

Standard Deviant Hot Tip

FOIL doesn't work for any other grouping of polynomials. *Remember* that you have to multiply each term in one set of parentheses by every one of the terms in the other set of parentheses. Count the terms you end up with before you simplify. There should be as many terms as the number of terms in one set of parentheses multiplied by the number of terms in the second set of parentheses. If there are fewer or more, go back and redo the multiplication. If there are the right number, all you have to do is hope your arithmetic is good and you didn't multiply the same two terms twice and forget another pair.

Section C: More Quadratics

`0:23:03`

A quadratic polynomial is the product of two first-degree polynomial expressions. Using FOIL, you can see that multiplying two linear polynomials will always result in one term with an exponent of 2. In other words, the answer is always a quadratic polynomial.

`0:23:36`

For example, $(3x - 1)(x + 2) = 3x^2 + 6x + (-x) - 2$
$$= 3x^2 + 5x - 2$$

A quadratic polynomial can always be put into this basic quadratic form. The equation $y = 3x^2 + 5x - 2$ reveals the pattern for the standard form for a quadratic equation:

$$y = ax^2 + bx + c$$

You using the
whole fist, doc?

- Irwin Fletcher

where a stands for the x^2 coefficient, b is the x coefficient, and c is the constant.

⊙ The standard form for a quadratic equation is similar to the standard form for a linear equation:

`0:24:08`

$$y = mx + b$$

⊙ The letters m and b are the traditional symbols for the slope and the y-intercept of a line, but any other letters work just as well.

STUDY SIDEKICK

⊙ Using b instead of m for the coefficient of x, and using c as the coefficient that has no x, the standard linear equation becomes $y = bx + c$.

⊙ A quadratic equation is like a linear equation except that it has another term: an x squared.

Remember...

⊙ Quadratics are square, so they are of the second degree.

⊙ With a linear equation, the slope (rate of change) is a constant represented by m.

⊙ Unlike linear equations, the rate of change for quadratic equations is not constant. In the practical world, quadratic equations are often used to model situations where the rate of change itself changes, so that the slope is different at different points on the graph.

One such situation is the position of a falling object accelerating due to gravity. We'll look closely at one gravity example to help relay this idea of how rates of change shift over time.

Check This Out...

In our example, position can be measured on the y-axis as how far the falling body is above the ground. As usual, the x-axis is used to show time.

The body starts out 100 feet above the ground. Scientists have found that in this context the equation for position and time is $y = 100 - 16x^2$. By choosing different values for x and using the equation to compute c, we can find points on the graph.

⊙ At time $x = 0$, the equation shows that y $= 100$.

That point on the graph indicates the starting point for the fall.

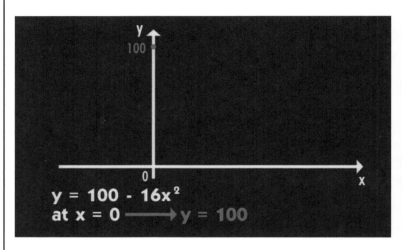

$y = 100 - 16x^2$
at $x = 0 \longrightarrow y = 100$

⊙ At time $x = 1$ second, the equation says $y = 100 - 16$ or 84. This gives us a point on the graph (1,84).

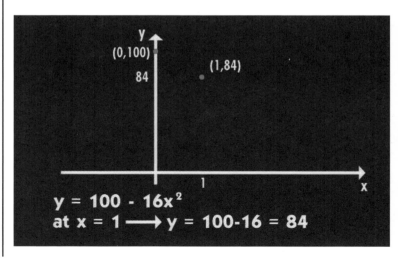

$y = 100 - 16x^2$
at $x = 1 \longrightarrow y = 100-16 = 84$

⊙ At time $x = 2$ seconds the equation says

$$y = 100 - (16)(2)^2$$

$$= 100 - 64$$

$$= 36$$

So $x = 2$ and $y = 36$

This gives us another point on the graph $(2, 36)$.

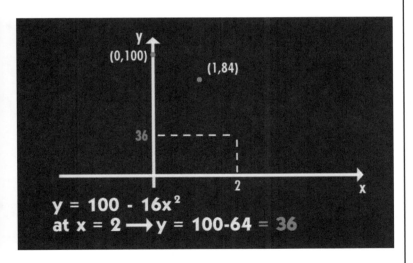

Now, these three points do not appear on a straight line. From $(0, 100)$ to $(1, 84)$, the object has fallen 16 feet in 1 second. So on the average, the object fell 16 feet per second.

That rate is the slope of the straight line joining the two points.

X = skier

Similarly, from (1, 84) to (2, 36) the object fell 48 feet in 1 second. On average, the object fell 48 feet per second, which is the slope between the two points.

Note that the rate is not the same for both calculations: first the object fell 16 feet per second, then it fell 48 feet per second. As expected, the falling object sped up. The fact that it speeds up means that you will not always see the same slope between any two points on the graph. The rate or slope itself changes over time.

We found a few points on the graph by using simple numbers for x: 0, 1, and 2. A better picture of the graph can be found by determining points using the same approach, but with xs like .37, 1.29, .03, and so on.

⊙ The resulting shape, as expected, is not a straight line.

Between different pairs of points on the graph, there will be different slopes or rates.

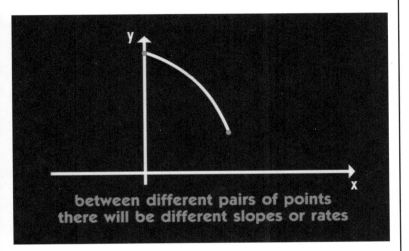

between different pairs of points
there will be different slopes or rates

⊙ Plotted all together, the points on the graph form a curve.

Section D: Graphs of Quadratic Equations

`0:24:19`

When graphed, a quadratic equation takes the form of a parabola.

⊙ The graph for the falling object we just saw is part of a parabola.

Famous parabolas include:

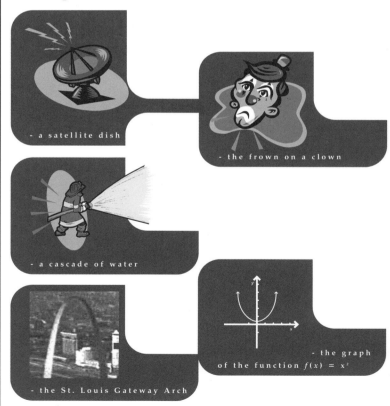

- a satellite dish

- the frown on a clown

- a cascade of water

- the graph of the function $f(x) = x^2$

- the St. Louis Gateway Arch

Not-so-famous parabolas include:

- Aunt Harriet's triple chin

- Uncle Hank's waist line

There are some great graphing calculators to help you do graphs of quadratic equations. Now we'll give you some good examples and details on the graphs of quadratic equations.

The graph of a quadratic equation is a curve that starts in one direction, turns, and then heads in the opposite direction. The point where the graph turns and changes direction is called the **vertex** (not to be confused with a **Kleenex**).

`0:27:28`

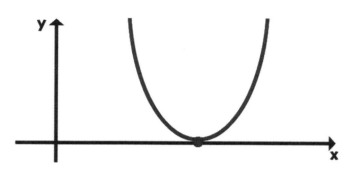

the point where the graph turns and changes direction - **vertex**

If you draw a vertical line through the vertex, you split the parabola into two symmetric halves. That vertical line is called the **axis of symmetry.**

`0:27:50`

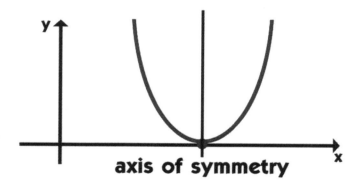

axis of symmetry

The values of the coefficients *a*, *b*, and *c* will dictate the exact form of the graph:

$$y = ax^2 + bx + c$$

Check This Out...

The value for *a* has a direct effect on both the width and direction of the parabola.

⊙ If the value for *a* is positive, or greater than 0, then the parabola opens upward and its vertex is at the bottom.

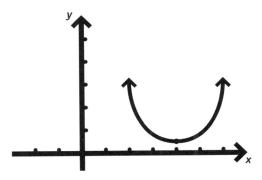

⊙ If the value of *a* is less than 0, or negative, the parabola opens downward and the vertex is at the top.

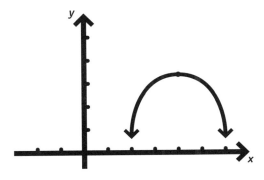

⊙ Also, the closer the value for *a* is to 0, the wider the parabola grows; and as *a* gets further away from 0, the parabola gets more and more narrow.

⊙ *a* cannot equal zero. If *a* were 0, we'd actually have a linear equation. Why? Because if *a* were zero, then ax^2 would also be zero. Which means that, in effect, there would effectively be no x^2 term at all. So all you'd have left is $bx + c$, which is just a linear expression.

Remember how in a linear equation $y = mx + b$, the value of *b* was the *y*-axis intercept? Well, conveniently, in a quadratic equation, the value for *c* is the *y*-axis intercept.

Look at what happens to a quadratic equation when $x = 0$:

$$y = a(0)^2 + b(0) + c = c$$

⊙ If $x = 0$, $y = c$ and the graph of the equation crosses the *y*-axis at *c*.

As a special case, when $c = 0$, the graph of the quadratic crosses the *y-axis* at 0.

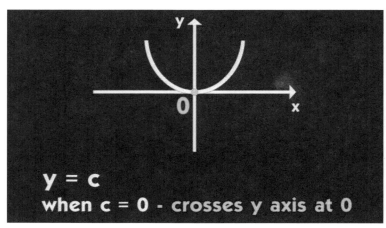

y = c
when c = 0 - crosses y axis at 0

Standard Deviant Hot Tip

- When $c = 0$, the graph of the equation crosses the y-axis at 0.

- For the equation $y = 3x^2 - 12x + 2$, the graph crosses the y-axis at 2 because $c = 2$.

- Remember: the graph intercepts the y-axis at c.

The axis of symmetry is a handy little line that can be found in handy equation form:

$$x = \frac{-b}{2a}$$

Let's look at an axis of symmetry example:

$$y = 3x^2 - 12x + 2$$

- The axis of symmetry is given by:

$$x = \frac{-b}{2a}$$

$$= -\frac{(-12)}{(2)(3)}$$

$$= 2$$

I see your schwartz is as big as mine.

- Dark Helmet

⊙ *Remember* that the axis of symmetry is a vertical line. x = 2 tells us where this vertical line crosses the *x*-axis.

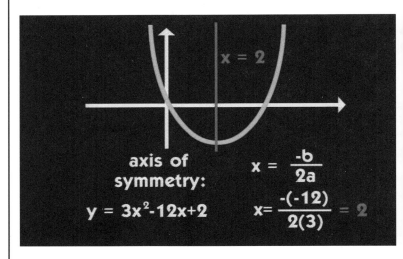

Remember, too, that the vertex of the graph, either the highest or lowest point, is always on the axis of symmetry. To find the vertex, we need both the *x* and the *y* values. We know the *x* is $\frac{-b}{2a}$ because the vertex is on the axis of symmetry. So, to find the *y* we use the standard equation:

$$y = ax^2 + bx + c$$

For the example $y = 3x^2 - 12x + 2$, we already found the axis of symmetry: $x = 2$.

⊙ Plug that x into the equation to find

$$y = 3(2)^2 - 12(2) + 2$$

$$y = -10$$

This gives the point $(2, -10)$, which is the vertex of the parabola.

Quiz 4

1. A square root can be written in two different ways. The square root of thirteen can be written as _____ or _____.

2. What are the square roots of: 1, 121, 4, 100, 9, 81, 16, 64, 25, 49, 36?

3. A binomial has _____ term(s).

4. What is:

    a. $(6x)^2$?

    b. $(4x - 3)^2$?

5.   a. What does FOIL stand for?

    b. When is it used?

6. Which of the following are in the standard form of a quadratic equation?

    a. $y = 3x - 12$

b. $4x^2 + y - 13 = 0$

c. $y = (x + 1)(2x - 7)$

d. $y = 3^{1\backslash 2}x^2 + 4x - 5$

7. When graphed, a quadratic equation takes the form of a

   _____.

8. A vertical line drawn through the vertex of the graph of a
   quadratic equation is called its _____.

9. Given $y = ax^2 + bx + c$,

   a. What is the y-intercept of the parabola?

   b. What is the equation for the axis of symmetry of
      the parabola?

10. Given $y = 4x^2 + 4x + 1$,

   a. What is the y-intercept?

   b. What is the axis of symmetry?

   c. Where is the vertex of this parabola?

Quadratic Roots and Factors

Just as with linear functions, the real roots of a quadratic function are where the graph of the function crosses the x-axis (the points at which $y = 0$).

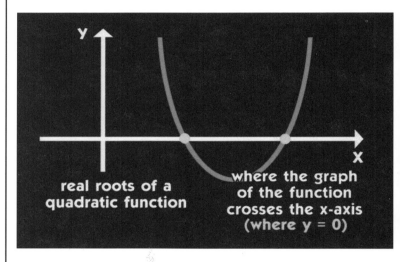

real roots of a quadratic function

where the graph of the function crosses the x-axis (where y = 0)

Since we already determined that the graph of a quadratic equation goes in one direction, then turns around and heads back in the direction it came from, the graph can cross the x-axis a maximum of two times.

Quadratic functions may therefore have *up to two real roots.*

However, the graph of a quadratic can simply touch the x-axis at its vertex.

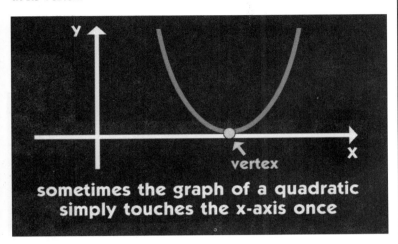

sometimes the graph of a quadratic simply touches the x-axis once

That's only one point. When the graph of a quadratic equation touches the x-axis at its vertex, *the equation has one real root.*

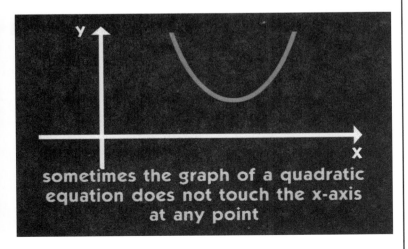

sometimes the graph of a quadratic equation does not touch the x-axis at any point

And the graph of the quadratic equation sometimes doesn't touch the *x*-axis at any point, ever. *These quadratic equations have no real roots.*

Do they wander rootless through the infinite algebraic wilderness forever? No. *Quadratic equations without real roots must have imaginary and complex roots.*

Video Notes

V2

Section A: Factoring Quadratic Equations

`0:30:00`

One way to find the real roots of an equation is to factor it. In factoring you break the equation down into the product of two binomial factors. Then all you do is set $y = 0$ and simply solve for x. Factoring a quadratic equation isn't necessarily a simple process and it can get quite complicated if, for instance, the coefficients are large. Sometimes the roots can't be expressed as exact fractions or finite decimals; factoring is impractical. But factoring is often the single simplest way to find the real roots of an equation, so let's see how it's done.

For example, take the expression:

$$x^2 + x - 6$$

Our mission is to find the two first-degree binomial factors which, when multiplied together, yield this expression as a product. So you're trying to find what two factors multiplied out give you $x^2 + x - 6$.

Finding the factors can be a brutal, exacting, trial-and-error process, and there are no shortcuts. And that's the way it is–sorry.

Before starting, let's review how two factors are multiplied using the FOIL method. Look at this example:

`0:31:42`

$$(3x - 4)(2x + 1) = 6x^2 - 5x - 4$$

⊙ Notice that 6, the coefficient of x^2, comes from multiplying the x coefficients from the two factors in parentheses ($3x$ and $2x$). These are the FIRST parts in FOIL.

⊙ Similarly, the final coefficient in the answer, -4, comes from the LAST parts of the factors (-4 and 1).

This pattern will occur every time you use FOIL.

`0:32:28`

Factoring is the reverse process of FOIL:

⊙ We start out knowing the answer in the form $6x^2 - 5x - 4$ and we want to find the two binomial factors that are in parentheses.

⊙ The point to keep in mind is this: the two FIRST coefficients have to multiply together to form 6, and the two LAST coefficients must multiply to equal -4.

Returning to the earlier problem, we want to factor

$$x^2 + x - 6.$$

Following the pattern just discussed:

⊙ The two FIRST coefficients have to multiply together to give the coefficient of x^2, which is 1.

⊙ And the two LAST coefficients in the parentheses have to multiply together to equal -6.

What are some possibilities? The FIRSTS could be 1 and 1 or -1 and -1. Either choice multiplies together to give 1. For the LASTS we can use -1 and 6 or -2 and 3. These can also be ordered differently and the minus sign can be repositioned in various ways. Just using the 2 and 3, for example, we have

$$2(-3) \quad (-2)3 \quad 3(-2) \quad (-3)2$$

These different combinations are all possibilities for the LAST coefficients.

Looking at both FIRSTS and LASTS there are many possibilities. Try one: make the FIRST coefficients 1 and 1 and make the LAST coefficients -1 and 6. That gives the factors $(x - 1)$ and $(x + 6)$.

Unfortunately, there is no guarantee that this choice is correct. How can you tell if it is? Multiply them using FOIL and see if you obtain the quadratic we started with which was:

$$x^2 + x - 6$$

Here it goes:

$$(x - 1)(x + 6) = x^2 + 6x - x - 6$$

$$= x^2 + 5x - 6$$

Unfortunately this is not quite what we were looking for, so the factors we tried were wrong. This is where the trial-and-error part of the process comes in.

You have to try different combinations of the FIRST and LAST coefficients and check whether each combination works using FOIL. Sometimes you get lucky and guess right on the first try.

Sometimes *none* of the combinations will work. But mostly you will find a combination that does work, and with practice you can get good at guessing which combinations to try.

Standard Deviant Hot Tip

Here's a handy factoring tip for you. If the c coefficient of the quadratic equation is positive, or:

$$ax^2 + bx + c$$

Then the sign inside the factors will be the same, either both positive or both negative, like so:

$$(+) (+)$$
$$(-) (-)$$

If the c coefficient is negative, then the signs in the factors will be different, or one positive and one negative:

$$(+) (-)$$

Okay, we still need to find the right factors for:

$$x^2 + x - 6$$

You can do this with your knowledge of factoring, just set up the frame-work.

We know that the coefficients of the x's in the factors must be 1 and 1, or,

$$(1x)\,(1x)$$

because the x^2 has a coefficient of the polynomial is **negative** 6. So, we know that one factor has to be x plus something, and one to be x minus something, or,

$$(x - \ )\,(x + \ )$$

Finally we know that the pair of numbers multiply to equal 6, which means that they are either:

$$1,6 \text{ or } 2,3$$

We tried -1 and $+6$, $(x + \_)(x + \_) = (x + 6)(x - 1)$

$$= x^2 + 5x - 6$$

Wrong!

⊙ For $+1$ and -6, $(x + \_)(x + \_) = (x + 1)(x - 6)$

$$= x^2 - 5x - 6$$

⊙ Finally, for -3 and $+2$, $(x + \_)(x + \_) = (x - 3)(x + 2)$

$$= x^2 - x - 6$$

Wrong! Close, but no cigar.

Through trial and error, we have found the factors for $x^2 + x - 6$. They are:

$$(x - 2) \text{ and } (x + 3).$$

Section B: Finding Roots from Factors

`0:38:16`

Once we find the factors, it's easy for us to determine the roots of the equation simply by setting each factor equal to 0.

Setting $x + 3 = 0$, we find that $x = -3$.

Similarly, setting $x - 2 = 0$, we find that $x = 2$

These two values, $x = 2$ and $x = -3$, both result in a final value of 0 when plugged into our equation. Therefore, the real roots of the quadratic equation $x^2 + x - 6 = 0$ are -3 and 2.

This trick always works:

- ☉ If $x = 3$ is a root, then $(x - 3)$ is a factor.

- ☉ If $x = -8$ is a root, then $[x - (-8)]$, which is the same as $(x + 8)$, is a factor.

- ☉ If $x = 346.287$ is a root, then $(x - 346.287)$ is a factor. You see the pattern, so here's the rule: *For any real number, if $x = r$ is a root, then $(x - r)$ is a factor.*

  You see the pattern, so here's the rule:

For any real number r, if $x = r$ is a root, then $(x - r)$ is a factor.

That guy's not unfaithful, he's frank and earnest... in Chicago, he's Frank, and in New York he's Earnest.

- Henny Youngman

> Through this rule you can see how factors and roots are intimately linked, kind of like love and marriage, law and order, country and western, Mork and Mindy.

You usually have to factor an equation to find the roots. Sometimes you'll have the roots and be able to use them to find the factors; we'll give an example of that later. The point is that in the rest of our examples we'll find both the factors and the roots. Ya don't get one without the other.

Since factoring is one of those things you'll do all the time in algebra, we'll do some more examples so you really get the hang of it.

How about the factors for $x^2 - 7x + 12$?

☉ What are the possibilities for FIRST coefficients? We'll start with 1 and 1 because that's easiest. Now what are the possibilities for LASTS? We need to choose numbers that will multiply together to result in 12. Some obvious choices are 1 and 12, 2 and 6, or 3 and 4.

☉ The first combination would be

$$(x + 1)(x + 12)$$

Does that give the desired result of $x^2 - 7x + 12$?

Using FOIL, we find $(x + 1)(x + 12) = x^2 + 13x + 12$. That's not what we want.

⊙ Next, try $(x + 2)(x + 6) = x^2 + 8x + 12$.

Wrong again.

⊙ What about $(x + 3)(x + 4) = x^2 + 7x + 12$?

Still no luck. But this is pretty close. It's just that the sign for $7x$ is wrong.

⊙ The correct answer is

$$(x - 3)(x - 4) = 5\,x^2 - 7x + 12.$$

Looking back at the guesses, we can see that using two positive numbers for our LASTS cannot possibly give a negative number for the combination of INSIDE and OUTSIDE parts. It would have been better to try negative numbers. Remember the tip from before: If the c coefficient is positive, the factors must be both positive or both negative. Practicing many factoring problems will lead you to a number of ideas like that and will help you make better choices for the combinations you try.

⊙Using the factors we found that:

$$x^2 - 7x + 12 = 0$$

can be rewritten in the form:

$$(x - 3)(x - 4) = 0.$$

The solutions are 3 and 4. How did we get that?

⊙ We set $(x - 3) = 0$, so $x = 3$.

⊙ Then we set $(x - 4) = 0$, so $x = 4$.

Here is one more example:

$$x^2 + 5x + 3$$

This time, there are not many choices for FIRSTS or LASTS.

⊙ Possible FIRSTS are 1 and 1 or -1 and -1

⊙ Possible LASTS are 1 and 3, 3 and 1, -1 and -3, or -3 and -1.

There are eight different possible combinations of FIRSTS and LASTS, and none of them work.

This is a problem for which factoring by trial and error doesn't work. A little later, there will be another method called the quadratic formula for solving the equation $x^2 + 5x + 3 = 0$. So keep it in mind!

As we said before, sometimes you happen to know a root for a quadratic, like if you discover a root while plotting points on a graph. You can use any roots you know to help factor the equation.

Here's an example:

$$y = 3x^2 + 2x - 5$$

⊙ One root is $x = 1$, and this goes with the factor $(x - 1)$. This is using the reverse logic from before. Instead of factoring first, then using the factors to find roots, this time we found a root, and then used it to make up a factor.

⊙ Now, knowing that $(x - 1)$ is a factor means there is a way to complete this equation: $(x - 1)$ times *what* x plus *what* equals $3x^2 + 2x - 5$, or in symbols:

$$(x - 1)(?x + ?) = 3x^2 + 2x + 5$$

⊙ The factoring problem can be approached through trial and error by looking at combinations for the FIRSTS and LASTS. But this time we already know one FIRST and one LAST. That reduces the amount of work, *big time*.

⊙ Since one FIRST is already known to be 1, the other one will have to be 3 because 3 times 1 must equal 3. Since one LAST is already known to be -1, the other one will have to be 5.

⊙ Check by multiplying:

$$(x - 1)(3x + 5) = 3x^2 + 2x - 5$$

⊙ Looking for roots, we set each factor equal to 0:

$$(x - 1) = 0$$

$$(3x + 5) = 0$$

⊙ The first factor gives us $x - 1 = 0$, or the root we already knew: $x - 1$.

⊙ The other factor gives us:

$$3x + 5 = 0$$

$$3x = -5$$

$$x = \frac{-5}{3}.$$

For this problem, the roots are 1 and $\frac{-5}{3}$. Great job!

Section C: Single-Root Quadratics

`0:45:27`

For a slightly different root-finding example, we'll look at a product we found already when we FOILed two first-order polynomials together:

$$y = 4x^2 + 4x + 1$$

Remember, we found $4x^2 + 4x + 1$ by multiplying $(2x + 1)(2x + 1)$. Let's find the real roots of this function. We set y to 0 since the graph of the equation will cross the x-axis when $y = 0$. So we have:

$$0 = (2x + 1)(2x + 1).$$

As with our other examples, for this equation to be true at least one of the factors must equal 0. Any time there are two factors, we can set either factor equal to 0 and solve for x.

In this instance the factors are the same: they are both $2x + 1$. This means that there will be only one root for the equation since solving for either factor will yield the same answer.

⊙ So we set the quantity $2x + 1$ equal to 0,

$$2x + 1 = 0$$

and simply solve for x. Isolating x on one side by itself, we get $2x = -1$, so $x = \frac{-1}{2}$ and our root is $\frac{-1}{2}$.

STUDY SIDEKICK

⊙ In this case, the quadratic equation only had one root.

We said before that when there is just one real root, the graph of the equation will touch the x-axis at just one point, and that point is the vertex. This means the vertex is the same point as the x-intercept.

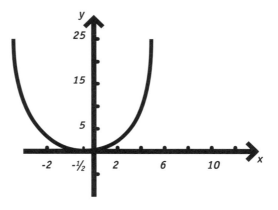

We know from before when we looked at the axis of symmetry that the x value for the vertex is given by

$$x = \frac{-b}{2a}$$

Standard Deviant Hot Tip

Remember that the vertex is the only point on the graph that sits on the axis of symmetry. Don't forget to look at your insert card for this and other fine algebraic formulas!

So this gives us another way to find these special one-root situations. Compute $x = \frac{-b}{2a}$ and then substitute that x into the quadratic equation to find the y coordinate of the vertex. If y comes out as 0, then you know $x = \frac{-b}{2a}$ is a root.

Remember…roots are on the x-axis, where $y = 0$. So it's the only root of the equation.

We can apply this idea to the preceding example:

$$y = 4x^2 + 4x + 1$$

Here, $a = 4$, $b = 4$, and $c = 1$.

⊙ The vertex occurs at

$$x = \frac{-b}{(2a)} = \frac{-4}{8}$$

or in this case

$$\text{so } x = \frac{-1}{2}.$$

⊙ Substituting that x into the equation, we see that:

$$y = 4\left(\frac{-1}{2}\right)^2 + 4\left(\frac{-1}{2}\right) + 1$$

$$y = 1 - 2 + 1 = 0.$$

⊙ Since $y = 0$, this proves that $x = \frac{-1}{2}$ is a root.

⊙ Since it's also the x for the vertex, it's the *only* root.

This jibes with what we saw earlier: When both factors are identical, there is only one single root for the equation. Often there are patterns to these one-root examples of quadratic equations, and it will make your life a lot easier if you can learn to recognize them.

Section D: Two Factoring Shortcuts (Kinda)

For binomial squares, here's a pattern for you:

In the trinomial version of each equation, if the c, or final constant, is a perfect square and the a coefficient is 1, then take the square root of c and double it.

If the square root of c times 2 equals the b or $-b$, then you know it's a single-root equation.

For example, take:

$$x^2 - 6x + 9.$$

You can see that 9 is a perfect square. The square root of 9 is 3, and 3 times 2 is 6. So you know that equation has only one root, like these:

Two other examples:

$$(x - 4)(x - 4) = x^2 - 8x + 16$$

$$(x + 2)(x + 2) = x^2 + 4x + 4$$

Or how about another example?

$$x^2 + 20x + 100$$

Also, you would recognize 100 as a perfect square. Its square root, 10, doubles to 20, so $x^2 + 20x + 100$ fits this same squaring pattern, and you know it has only one single root, or:

$$(x + 10)(x + 10)$$

This trinomial has the same pattern:

$$x^2 + 10x + 25$$

The final constant is a perfect square, 25.

Take the square root of that amount, which gives you 5, and then double it. The result is 10, which is the b coefficient.

That tells us that $x^2 + 10x + 25$ factors into two identical parts and even tells us what the parts are. The constant term for each part is 5, which we squared to find 25. So...

$$x^2 + 10x + 25 = (x + 5)(x + 5)$$

⊙ The equation $x^2 + 10x + 25 = 0$ has just one root,

$$x = -5$$

Hey babe, that polynomial only has one root, so do you want to come over to my place or what?

The equation has two roots. It's just that both roots equal 25, so sometimes we casually (and incorrectly) say there is only one root. This is a good trivia question. Who knows where you might use this bit of titillating trivia, but it's interesting nonetheless.

There are many patterns that can help reveal special kinds of factors. The best way to discover these patterns is to do many factoring and FOILing problems.

We've got one more handy pattern that will let you factor equations more easily if you can recognize it.

When there is no x term, that is, no middle or b coefficient term, and when the other two coefficients are both perfect squares like 49 or 25, there is a simple pattern to the factors.

Check out this example:

$$x^2 - 49 = (x + 7)(x - 7)$$

⊙ You can use FOIL to check:

$$(x + 7)(x - 7) = x^2 - 7x + 7x - 49$$

$$= x^2 - 49.$$

⊙ Notice how the $7x$ terms effectively cancel each other and how the final constant is always a negative perfect square.

STUDY SIDEKICK

A prisoner is placed inside of a jail cell. The cell is bolted shut, there are no windows, no bars, and no holes any where. the only things in his jail cell are a bed, and a mirror. That's it, yet he escapes easily. HOW? (for the answer read ahead)

Another example:

$$x^2 - 36 = (x + 6)(x - 6)$$

$$x^2 - 1 = (x + 1)(x - 1)$$

$$4x^2 - 9 = (2x + 3)(2x - 3).$$

In each case, the two factors look the same except that one has a plus sign and the other has a minus sign between the terms. The FIRST values are both equal to the square root of the x^2 term, while the LAST values are each the square root of the last term (a constant in these examples). All you need to do is put a plus between them in one factor and a minus between them in the other.

Let's take the equation:
$$y = 16x^2 - 100$$

If you have to factor it and find the roots, this pattern makes it easy. If you want to find the roots (x intercepts), you can follow the pattern and see that $16x^2$ and 100 are both perfect squares with square roots of $4x$ and 10.

⊙ So you first factor $16x^2 - 100$ into:

$$(4x - 10) \text{ and } (4x + 10).$$

⊙ That makes the equation:

$$y = (4x - 10)(4x + 10)$$

⊙ Now set $y = 0$ since we want to find the roots:

$$(4x - 10)(4x + 10) = 0$$

⊙ Finally, set each factor equal to 0 and solve for x:

$$4x - 10 = 0$$

$$4x = 10$$

$$x = \frac{10}{4} \text{ or } x = \frac{5}{2}$$

Let $\qquad 4x + 10 = 0,$

$$4x = -10,$$

$$x = \frac{-10}{4} \text{ or } x = \frac{-5}{2}$$

The results are $\qquad x = \dfrac{5}{2} \text{ and } x = \dfrac{-5}{2}$

⊙ Check this by substituting your roots back into the equation to see whether you still get zero when you're finished with the arithmetic and…you're done!

You may discover other shortcuts as you practice factoring and FOILing in class and in your assignments. Now remember not to play with your FOIL too much. The most important way to factor is by trial and error, even if it's kind of a pain. And if THAT kind of factoring doesn't work, then you can always resort to… **bobsledding!** Well, not really. Actually you can always resort to the quadratic formula.

0:55:09

Section E: The Quadratic Formula

As we said, it is not always practical or possible to factor an equation. But it is always possible to find the roots of a quadratic equation by the use of another method: the *quadratic formula.*

Remember that for linear equations, we found the formula for the root of a linear equation to be $\frac{-b}{m}$ when the form of the equation was $y = f(x) = mx + b$. For quadratic equations, the root-finding formula is just a bit more complicated.

The quadratic formula is

$$x = \frac{-b \pm \sqrt{b^2 - 4ac}}{2a}$$

154

Or, in other words: *x equals negative b plus or minus the square root of the quantity b squared minus 4ac, all divided by 2a.* Yeah, it looks nasty. But don't stress, it's as easy as counting moose in a room with only two moose.

Hello, count
on us.

> Remember that the quadratic formula ALWAYS works for EVERY quadratic. By plugging in the values of the coefficients for *a*, *b*, and *c*, you can always come up with the roots of a quadratic equation. Again, using this method of quadratic magic you may find one, two, or zero real roots.

Okay, remember the equation we failed to factor before? It was $y = x^2 + 5x + 3$, and we couldn't factor it. Well, now we can find its roots. You use the quadratic formula for finding roots of equations that you can't factor any other way.

`0:56:00`

⊙ To find the roots of our equation, we must first set

$$y = 0, \text{ as in } x^2 + 5x + 3 = 0$$

⊙ In our equation, $a = 1$, $b = 5$, and $c = 3$. Now to make things a little easier, before we substitute all these into the quadratic formula, let's just compute the part inside the square root sign (or radical sign):

$$= \sqrt{b^2 - 4ac}$$

$$= \sqrt{5^2 - (4)(1)(3)}$$

155

STUDY SIDEKICK

$$= \sqrt{25 - 12}$$

$$= \sqrt{13}$$

⊙ Now the rest of the formula will be easier to manage.

We have

$$x = \frac{-5 \pm \sqrt{13}}{(2)(1)}$$

$$= \frac{-5 \pm \sqrt{13}}{2}$$

Of course, that is really two answers:

$$\frac{-5 + \sqrt{13}}{2} \quad \text{or} \quad \frac{-5 - \sqrt{13}}{2}$$

These can't be expressed exactly as a decimal or fractional form. If you want, you can compute accurate decimal approximations with a calculator. If you do, remember to add or subtract $\sqrt{13}$ from -5 first, and then divide that result by 2.

⊙ Rounding to 6 decimal places, we get $x = -4.302776$ and $x = -0.697224$. (But normally you can just leave the answers in radical form.)

So the quadratic formula helps you solve those equations you just can't factor. By the way, these roots can now be used to factor the original equation. As we saw, if you know a root, then x minus that root is a factor.

In this case, we have

$$x^2 + 5x + 3 = (x + 4.302776)(x + 0.697224)$$

The only way to give an exact factorization is to leave the square root of 13 in symbolic form in the answer:

$$x^2 + 5x + 3 = \left(x + \frac{-5 + \sqrt{13}}{2}\right)\left(x - \frac{-5 - \sqrt{13}}{2}\right)$$

You can see why factoring this equation by the trial-and-error methods used earlier is sort of impractical.

The **discriminant** is the name given to the value under the square root in the quadratic equation:

$$b^2 - 4ac$$

In the example we just did, the discriminant was 13. The discriminant is so-called because it lets us discriminate with some at-a-glance insight between quadratics with zero, one, or two real roots. After you substitute the values of a, b, and c into the quadratic formula, if the value of the discriminant is *positive*, the equation has *two* real roots.

If this value is 0, as it sometimes is, there is *one* real root. And if the value of the discriminant is *negative,* then you know immediately that the quadratic equation has *no* real roots.

Remember…

- ⊙ If the discriminant is positive, the quadratic equation has two real roots.

- ⊙ If it's zero, there's only one real root.

- ⊙ And if the discriminant is negative, there are no real roots.

These generalizations are possible because the quadratic formula takes the square root of the discriminant. A square root of any positive number yields two answers, one positive and one negative. And the square root of zero yields one answer, since the only number times itself that will equal zero is zero.

So if the square root of a positive number gives two real answers and the square root of zero gives one real answer, zero, then what do you get for the square root of a negative number?

Ah, yes, square roots of negative numbers. What is the square root of a negative number? The problem we run into here is the inconvenient fact that no real number multiplied by itself will ever give you a negative number. Never, not ever. So what can you do when your discriminant is negative and you have to take its square root? Well…let us formally introduce: **imaginary numbers.**

Section F: Imaginary Numbers

1:03:18

To represent imaginary numbers, mathematicians use the number or symbol i.

1:03:30

$$i \text{ is defined as } \sqrt{-1} \text{ or } (-1)^{\frac{1}{2}}$$

Another way of saying this is: i squared, or multiplied by itself, equals negative one:

$$i^2 = -1$$

Even though it's a letter, i is not a variable. Also, it's not a real number—it cannot be found anywhere on the number line. It exists only in the mathematical mind, and now it's inside yours...yee haw!

So why is it so important? *Because i can be used to make other numbers with negative squares.*

⊙ For example: $(3i)^2 = (3i)(3i) = (9)(i^2) = -9$

⊙ Similarly, $(4i)^2 = -16$, $(5i)^2 = -25$...you get the idea.

⊙ And, just as the equation $i^2 = -1$ can be expressed in the form $i = \sqrt{-1}$, the equation $(3i)^2 = -9$ can be written as $3i = \sqrt{-9}$.

⊙ Similarly:

$$\sqrt{-16} = 4i,$$

$$\sqrt{-25} = 5i,$$

$$\sqrt{-36} = 6i, \text{ and so on.}$$

Rule...

1. To take the square root of a negative number, throw away the negative sign and take a square root in the usual way.

2. Next, multiply the answer by *i*.

Don't forget, the most important thing to remember is the square root of negative 1 equals *i*, or

$$\sqrt{-1} = i$$

To take a slightly more complicated example, we can look for the square root of -20 (or $\sqrt{-20}$):

Now $\sqrt{20} = (\sqrt{4})(\sqrt{5})$.

The $\sqrt{4}$ simplifies to 2.

So $\sqrt{20}$ simplifies to $2\sqrt{5}$.

Thanks to the imaginary number i, taking the square root of -20 is not that much more complicated. In this case, the factors of $\sqrt{-20}$ are $\sqrt{4}$, $\sqrt{5}$, and $\sqrt{-1}$ or i.

◉ Simplifying the $\sqrt{4}$ to 2 and the $\sqrt{-1}$ to i, we come up with $2i\sqrt{5}$.

◉ Or, to put it another way, $(2i\sqrt{5})^2 = -20$.

Standard Deviant Hot Tip

REMINDER: Don't confuse the square root of a negative number ($\sqrt{-a}$) with the negative square root of a positive number or, ($-\sqrt{a}$). Remember that any positive real number has two potential square roots: one that is positive and one that is negative. For example:

$$\sqrt{16} = \pm 4).$$

$$-\sqrt{16} = -4).$$

But the square root of negative 16 is 4 times the square root of -1, or i, giving you $4i$:

$$\sqrt{-16} = 4\sqrt{-1}$$

$$= 4i$$

And if you want to get silly, (okay, not incredibly silly) consider this. There are also two square roots of -16: $4i$ and *negative 4i*.

Now that you have been initiated into the world of imaginary numbers, you can see how all numbers are of three basic types:

1. **Real numbers**, which are the basic numbers you know and love so well.

2. **Imaginary numbers**, your new and abstract friends.

3. **Complex numbers**, which have had a messed-up childhood. Actually, they're just a combination of real and imaginary numbers. For example:

$$3 + 4i \qquad \frac{1}{2} - \frac{2}{3}i \qquad .7 + 1.3i$$

are all complex numbers.

A purely real number, one with no i part, can be written in a complex form: you can write 7.2 in the form $7.2 + 0i$. Why write anything in a more complex form than you have to? Well, sometimes you might have to combine a real number with a complex number. Similarly, a purely imaginary number, one in the form $12i$, can be put in the complex form $0 + 12i$.

This shows that all three types of numbers, real, imaginary and complex, can all be part of the form $a + bi$. Anything in that form is called a complex number. If $b = 0$, $a + bi$ is a purely real number; if $a = 0$, $a = bi$ is a purely imaginary number.

Roots of quadratic equations found using the quadratic formula may be purely real, purely imaginary, or a complex form that combines real and imaginary numbers.

`1:08:35`

Section G: A Practical Example

One of the most common applications of quadratic equations in the real world is finding the speed of falling objects. Here's an example. There is a special equation that models the position of falling objects in relation to time:

$$y = \frac{-1}{2} gx^2 + vx + h$$

⊙ First, let's define the variables and constants we are using. The constants in this equation are g, v, and h.

⊙ The value g stands for the *acceleration* of gravity. No matter where you are on the surface of the Earth, the acceleration of gravity is constant at 9.8 meters (or the American equivalent, 32 feet) per second squared. The acceleration of gravity is 9.8 meters (or 32 feet) per second squared.

The "squared" part happens this way: Speed is measured in meters per second (or feet per second). Acceleration tells how speed changes. Speed gets faster by 9.8 meters per second every second. This constant will be the same in every equation like this for Earth gravity.

⊙ The value v stands for the initial velocity. Initial velocity is the velocity of the object when its position is first measured, that is, when time, the x variable, still equals 0.

⊙ The value h stands for the initial height. The initial height is the height of the object when its position is first measured.

⊙ The dependent variable *y* stands for the height in relation to the independent variable *x*, the time that has passed.

How about an example?!

For our example, Galileo Galilei stands on the edge of a cliff 122.5 meters high with a bowling ball. He drops it off the edge. How long will it take the bowling ball to hit the ground below? Using the function that we now know describes the relationship between the position of a falling object and time, we can answer this question:

$$y = -\frac{1}{2}gx^2 + vx + h$$

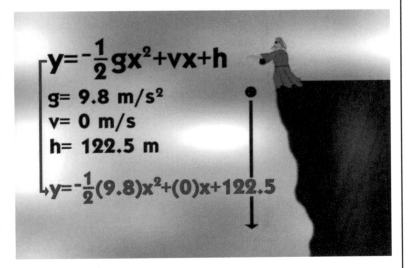

First, we must identify the constants:

⊙ The height we are dealing with is measured in meters, so the value for g we use is 9.8 meters per second squared. Galileo does not throw the bowling ball, he simply drops it, so the initial velocity v is 0 meters per second. And since the ball is dropped from a height of 122.5 meters, the initial height, or h, is 122.5 m.

⊙ Plugging these values into the equation, we get

$$y = \left(\frac{-1}{2}\right)(9.8)x^2 + (0)x + 122.5$$

This simplifies to

$$y = -4.9x^2 + 122.5$$

Now the variable y represents height of the ball in relation to time x.

⊙ We want to know how long it will take until the ball hits the ground, which is where the height $y = 0$. So we must find the time, x, when the height $y = 0$. To find x when $y = 0$....Wait a minute, that's a root!

⊙ In effect, we want to find the roots of the quadratic equation $y = 24.9x^2 + 122.5$. There are a couple of different ways we can do this. Let's try the quadratic formula.

⊙ In this quadratic equation, the coefficients are $a = -4.9$, $b = 0$, and $c = 122.5$. We can plug these values into the quadratic formula to find the roots of the equation.

$$x = \frac{-b \pm \sqrt{b^2 - 4ac}}{2a}$$

Since $a = -4.9$

$$b = 0$$

$$c = 122.5$$

This gives us:

$$x = \frac{-0 \pm \sqrt{0^2 - 4(-4.9)(122.5)}}{(2)(-4.9)}$$

or

$$x = \frac{\sqrt{(-4)(-4.9)(122.5)}}{-9.8}$$

$$x = \frac{\pm\sqrt{2401}}{-9.8}$$

$$x = \frac{\pm 49}{-9.8}$$

$$x = \pm 5.$$

⊙ The value of x cannot be negative because when Galileo drops the ball, the time is $x = 0$, so $x = -5$ would mean that the bowling ball hits the ground 5 seconds *before* he drops it. Illogical. So the bowling ball hits the ground 5 seconds **after** it is dropped.

We could give you about sixteen more examples of how to translate practical and word problems into algebraic equations, but we've still got some ground to cover. The fact is, if you know how to find the roots of any quadratic equation, either by factoring, using the quadratic formula, or solving for x, then you can solve any quadratic story problem as long as you plug your numbers into the right places. If you're unclear on factoring the quadratic formula, solving for x or anything else about quadratics, just flip to the beginning of this part of the book and read it again! Or watch the video again!

Quiz 5

1. A quadratic equation may have a maximum of _____ real root(s), which is where the graph of the equation touches the ____−axis.

2. When you break a quadratic equation down into the product of two binomials, you are _____ it.

3. Find the factors of $x^2 + x - 12$.

4. If a factor of an equation is $(x - r)$, then a root of the same equation is _____.

5. Find the roots of $3x^2 + 7x + 4 = 0$.

6. Find the roots of $x^2 - 22x = -121$ by factoring.

7. Given $4x^2 + 20x + 25$,

    a. The name of this expression is _____.

    b. The factors of this expression are _____.

8. Find the roots of $4x^2 + 20x + 36 = 11$.

9. Given $144 - 49x^2$.

    a. The name of this expression is _____.

    b. The factors of this expression are _____.

10. The quadratic formula can be used for all quadratic equations after they have been put into _____ form, which is _____.

11. Given $y = x^2 - 3x + 1$, use the quadratic formula to find its root(s).

12. An imaginary number is represented by the symbol _____, which is defined as _____.

13. A complex number is a combination of _____ and _____ numbers.

14. Given $y = x^2 + 3x + 3$, use the quadratic formula to find its root(s).

15.   a. Is $y = ax^2 + bx + c$ a quadratic equation? Is it a function?

    b. Is $x = ay^2 + by + c$ a quadratic equation? Is it a function?

Polynomials

1:14:50

The algebraic universe grows ever more vast and complicated and the creatures and equations in it grow ever stranger. We have dealt with linear equations of the form

$$y = mx + b$$

and quadratic equations of the form

$$y = ax^2 + bx + c.$$

Continuing our search for the most complex equation in the known universe, we now turn our attentions to another algebraic mutant beast, cousin to the quadratic equation: the **polynomial.**

`1:15:45`

Section A: General Polynomials

We already told you about polynomials, but in case you forgot, here's a flashback. These expressions and functions are all polynomials:

$$3x^{12} + 5x^7$$

$$4x^4 + x^2 + 5$$

$$f(x) = 8x^3 + x^2 + 2$$

$$f(x) = 3x^7 + 5x^{12} + x^3.$$

172

We have seen general forms for linear polynomials and quadratic polynomials. In a similar way, the standard form for a higher-degree polynomial has monomial terms made up of coefficients and powers of x. The terms are ordered so that the powers of x are decreasing.

Some examples are

$$-7x^3 + 2x - 1$$

$$x^5 - 2x^4 + 3x^3 - 5x^2 + 2x - 1$$

$$x^{20} + x^5 + x^3$$

We won't give each coefficient a different letter like we did for linear and quadratic standard forms, but we do have some things to say about two special coefficients.

The coefficient for the highest power of x, which is assumed not to be 0, is called the **leading coefficient**. In our first example, $-7x^3 + 2x - 1$, the leading coefficient equals -7. That coefficient goes with x^3, so this polynomial has a degree of 3. Similarly the last example, $x^{20} + x^5 + x^3$, is a degree-20 polynomial. Its leading coefficient is 1.

`1:17:13`

The other major coefficient is the last one in the expression, the one with no x in it (that is, the one with the ghost x to the zero power). This is called the constant term or the constant coefficient. We've seen it before as the y-intercept. So in our first example $-7x^3 + 2x - 1$, the constant term equals -1. In the example, $x^{20} + x^5 + x^3$, no constant term is present, so we say the constant term is 0.

`1:17:41`

1:17:57

Section B: Multiplying Polynomials

You also know, because we said it before, that polynomial expressions can be multiplied together using a modified form of the FOIL method. FOIL basically uses the distributive and commutative properties to distribute the terms from one of the polynomials being multiplied to the other.

Let's multiply the two polynomials

$$(x^2 - 3x + 1) \text{ and } (2x^3 + 4x^2 + 7x)$$

⊙ First, we'll multiply each term in the first expression by every term in the second expression. So we multiply $x^2(2x^3 + 4x^2 + 7x)$, then do the same with $-3x$ and 1. This gives us:

$$(x^2 - 3x + 1)(2x^3 + 4x^3 + 7x)$$

$$= x^2(2x^3 + 4x^2 + 7x) - 3x(2x^3 + 4x^2 + 7x)$$

$$+ 1(2x^3 + 4x^2 + 7x)$$

You look at me,
and suddenly
I'm in your arms.

- Joanie and
Chachi

⊙ Multiplying out all factors eventually yields

$$= x^2(2x^3 + 4x^2 + 7x) - 3x(2x^3 + 4x^2 + 7x) + 1(2x^3 + 4x^2 + 7x)$$

$$= 2x^5 + 4x^4 - 6x^4 + 7x^3 - 12x^3 + 2x^3 - 21x^2 + 4x^2 + 7x.$$

174

⊙ Simplifying and combining all terms of like degree, we finally get:

$$(x^2 - 3x + 1)(2x^3 + 4x^2 + 7x)$$

$$= 2x^5 - 2x^4 - 3x^3 - 17x^2 + 7x$$

These are a lot of calculations and you must be careful to carry though any negative signs and to simplify correctly. Or else...AAAALLLL that work is wrong and wasted. Especially when something takes a lot of work, it's really clever to do it right the first time, so you can go off and do other, cooler things...like yoga.

Polynomials can also be factored or divided. Just like with quadratic equations, the roots of a polynomial function can be found by determining its factors. Finding the factors of a polynomial can be a long, complicated, messy, ugly process, but you're gonna be obliged to do it on your tests... so you'd better learn it.

Section C: Factoring Polynomials

One way to find factors of a polynomial is through a form of algebraic long division that looks suspiciously like the long division you learned as a kid. Only harder.

⊙ For example let's try to see if $x - 3$ is a factor of

$$x^3 - 7x - 6.$$

⊙ When dividing $x - 3$ into $x^3 - 7x - 6$, set up the problem like a long division problem from elementary school. That is, you are dividing $x - 3$ into $x^3 + 0x^2$ (since there is no second–degree term) $- 7x - 6$.

So:

$$x - 3 \overline{)x^3 + 0x^2 - 7x - 6}$$

Now you must ask yourself, "What times x gives me x^3?"

⊙ Of course, it's x^2, so you write x^2 as the first part of the quotient and then multiply $x - 3$ by x^2, which gives you $x^3 - 3x^2$. Subtract this from $x^3 + 0x^2$ and you get $3x^2$. Bringing down the next term, $- 7x$, you would have $3x^2 - 7x$, like this:

$$
\begin{array}{r}
x^2 \\
x - 3 \overline{)x^3 - 0x^2 - 7x - 6} \\
\underline{x^3 - 3x^2 } \\
+3x^2 - 7x
\end{array}
$$

⊙ Now we begin again, dividing $x - 3$ into $3x^2 - 7x$. By just looking at the first terms, we see that x goes into $3x^2$ exactly $3x$ times, so $3x$ is the next part of the answer. Multiply $x - 3$ by $3x$, which gives us $3x^2 - 9x$. Subtracting, you're left with $2x - 6$, like this:

$$\begin{array}{r}
x^2 + 3x \\
x - 3 \overline{)x^3 - 0x^2 - 7x - 6} \\
\underline{x^3 - 3x^2 } \\
+3x^2 - 7x \\
\underline{+3x^2 - 9x } \\
+2x - 6
\end{array}$$

⊙ Now we see that $x - 3$ divides evenly into $2x - 6$ two times. So the solution to the long division problem $x^3 - 7x - 6$ divided by $x - 3$ equals $x^2 + 3x + 2$.

$$\begin{array}{r}
x^2 + 3x + 2 \\
x - 3 \overline{)x^3 - 0x^2 - 7x - 6} \\
\underline{x^3 - 3x^2 } \\
+3x^2 - 7x \\
\underline{+3x^2 - 9x } \\
+2x - 6 \\
\underline{+2x - 6} \\
0
\end{array}$$

⊙ Since $x - 3$ divides into $3x^2 - 7x - 6$ evenly without a remainder, $x - 3$ is a factor of $3x^2 - 7x - 6$. The quotient, $(x^2 + 3x + 2)$, is a factor of $x^3 - 7x - 6$ as well. We now know that $x^3 - 7x - 6 = (x - 3)(x^2 + 3x + 2)$.

⊙ The quadratic expression $x^2 + 3x + 2$ can be factored into $(x + 1)(x + 2)$, so $x^3 - 7x - 6 = (x - 3)(x + 1)(x + 2)$.

⊙ Setting the factored form of the expression $x^3 - 7x - 6$ equal to zero, we get: $0 = (x - 3)(x + 1)(x + 2)$.

So $x - 3 = 0$, $x + 1 = 0$, or $x + 2 = 0$.

Solving all of these equations for x, we get $x = 3$, $x = -1$, and $x = -2$.

The roots to the equation $x^3 - 7x - 6 = 0$ are 3, -1, and -2.

Note that there are **three** roots for this third–degree equation. You remember that the quadratic, or second-degree, equations we looked at always had (at most) two roots. A fourth-degree equation would have four or fewer roots and so on. The degree of a polynomial equation always limits the number of roots. *A polynomial can never have more roots than its degree.*

`1:24:00`

Summarizing the long division process for a third-order polynomial:

1. First, find a partial quotient of x^2 by dividing x into x^3 to get x^2.

2. Multiply x^2 by the divisor and subtract the product from the dividend.

3. Repeat the process until you either "clear it out" or reach a reminder.

178

Section D: Properties of Polynomial Graphs

While graphs of polynomial equations will obviously be different from one to the next, they will always fall into one of two general categories, which we will now demonstrate. *All polynomials have either even or odd degrees.* If you look at the following expressions, *linear expressions* (which have a degree of 1) and *quadratic expressions* (which have a degree of 2), you will see the following basic differences. The degree of a polynomial equation dictates the shape of the graph of the polynomial.

⊙ *Even-degree polynomials* will always resemble the shape of the quadratic parabola, which you are familiar with:

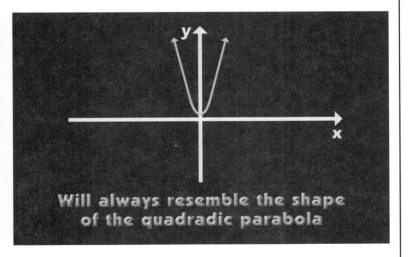

Will always resemble the shape of the quadradic parabola

They will either look like a scoop or an arch, possibly with a few little wrinkles somewhere in the middle.

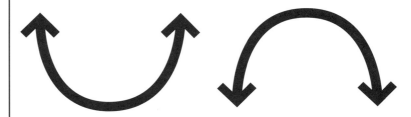

⊙ *Odd-degree equations* will always look, well, odd. Either positively odd or negatively odd.

Odd degree equations

Odd degree equations

Here's some more details. Any polynomial equation with an even value for its degree (like x^2, x^4, x^6, x^8...) will have a graph like a quadratic equation because it will hook around and exit the graph in roughly the same direction it entered from. Even-degree polynomial equations will look like either a scoop or an arch.

Any polynomial equation with an odd value for its degree (x^1, x^3, x^5, x^7...) will have graphs most similar to third-degree or cubic equations, in that they are curved. But they are also like first-degree or linear equations because they always exit the graph in the opposite direction from the one they entered. So they will always be, well, swoosh-like.

The simplest polynomials—single monomials such as x^3, x^4, x^5, and so on—illustrate these ideas. Also, notice that the higher the degree is, the thinner and steeper the graph becomes.

Here is a plot of $y = x^3$:

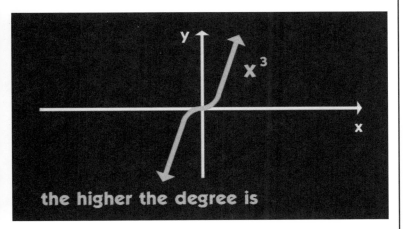

This is $y = x^5$:

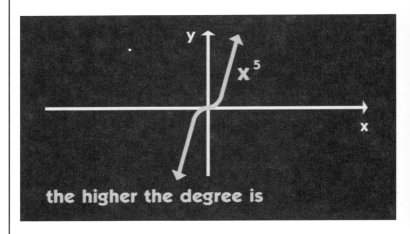

the higher the degree is

This is $y = x^7$:

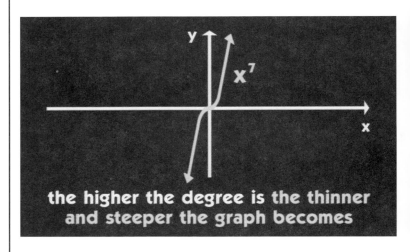

the higher the degree is the thinner
and steeper the graph becomes

And here is $y = x^9$:

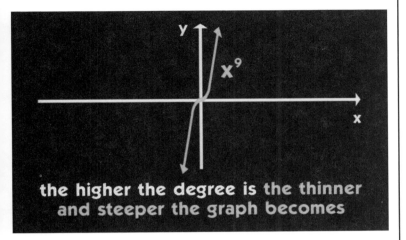

the higher the degree is the thinner and steeper the graph becomes

Miss Piggy,
you're on five.

-Scooter

It's important to recognize that for large values of x, high powers of x are so much larger than the lower powers that only the highest power will have much effect on the graph.

⊙ To demonstrate this, compare the terms $2x^4$ and $50x^2$. For $x = 100$, the first term, $2x^4$, is 200 million, and the second term, $50x^2$, is only 500 thousand. Now compared with 200 million, 500 thousand is small potatoes.

For even larger values of x, the effect is even more pronounced.

The point is this: For large enough values of x, you can ignore all but the highest degree term of the polynomial with little impact on the value of y. That means that for really large values of x, the graph of a polynomial must behave like a graph of the form $y = ax^n$, where n represents the highest degree term present in the polynomial.

183

⊙ As a specific example, if you want a general idea of what the graph of $y = 4x^5 - 3x^3 + 2x^2 + 7$ will look like for large values of x, just look at the first term $y = 4x^5$.

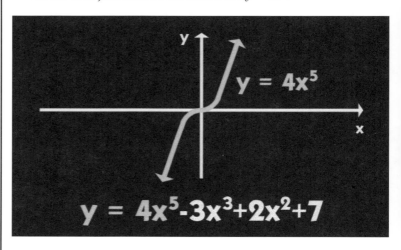

This is what $y = 4x^5 - 3x^3 + 2x^2 + 7$ actually looks like:

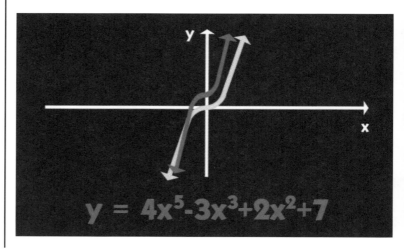

Also, just like with quadratic equations, the values of the coefficients for the first and last terms of a polynomial equation will influence the shape of the graph of that polynomial.

`1:29:51`

For example, let's see what happens to the graph when our leading coefficients are either positive or negative.

Look at these examples with even exponents and positive coefficients. You can see what happens to the graphs when the coefficients are made negative: The graphs flip over.

`1:30:28`

Here are graphs of $y = 4x^4$:

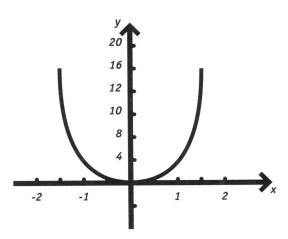

and $y = -4x^4$:

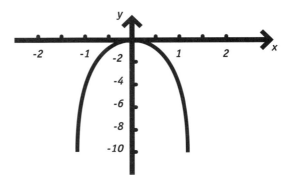

Finally, here is the graph of $y = 3x^2$:

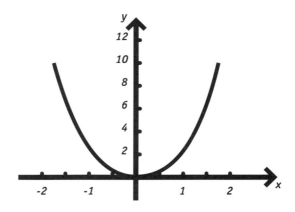

and here is the graph of $y = -3x^2$:

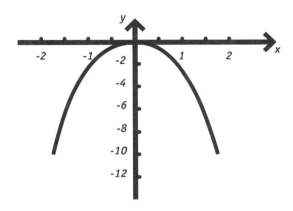

The next day Billy came home and said, "Mommy look, I learned how to draw a fork."

Now look at some graphs of equations with odd exponents and positive leading coefficients. Again, see what happens when the coefficients are made negative? You can see the general patterns.

Here is the graph of $y = .4x^3$:

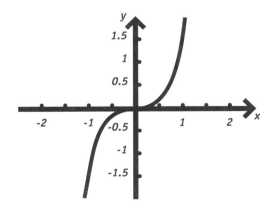

And here is the graph of $y = -.4x^3$:

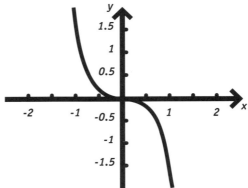

And the next day Billy came home and said, "Mommy look, I learned how to draw a table."

Now look at $y = .2x^5$:

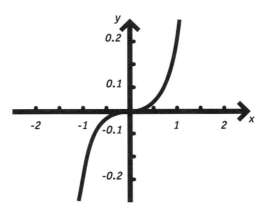

and compare that with the graph of $y = -.2x^5$ below:

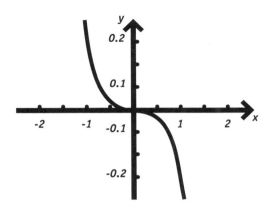

Okay, these generalities about the first term of a polynomial apply to the general shape of the graph, especially the parts far away from the y-axis. But right at the y-axis you can get other useful information. In fact, you can read the graph's y-intercept right off the end of the equation.

The constant is the y-intercept for any polynomial, same as it was for any linear or quadratic. This is true because the y-intercept is the point on the graph where $x = 0$, and when $x = 0$, all the terms of the polynomial that include an x will be 0 (because anything multiplied by 0 is 0), except for the final term, which has no x.

`1:31:14`

⊙ For example, if $y = 4x^4 + 3x^2 - 6x + 5$,

  then for $x = 0$, $y = 4(0) + 3(0) - 6(0) + 5$.

  So $y = 5$.

So you can see that whatever the last coefficient in the equation is, that's where the graph crosses the *y*-axis, no matter what the rest of the equation looks like.

On the last day Billy was so excited to show his mommy what he had learned… "Look, Mommy, I drew an elephant taking a bath!" Turn this page upside down and view his creation. ….Now back to algebra.

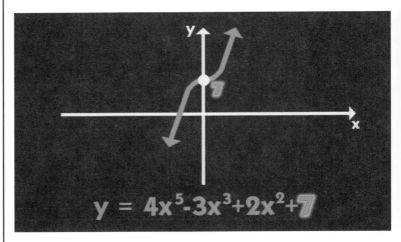

$$y = 4x^5 - 3x^3 + 2x^2 + 7$$

And if there is no constant, the *y*-intercept is 0 and the curve goes through point the origin (0, 0).

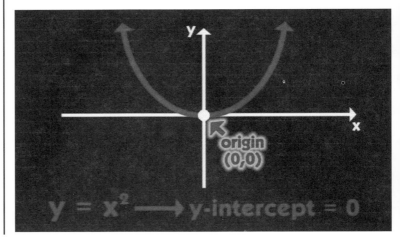

origin (0,0)

$$y = x^2 \longrightarrow y\text{-intercept} = 0$$

Polynomials tend to wiggle around a little bit somewhere in the center of the graph, but they can't wiggle too much. The degree places a limit on the number of wiggles.

⊙ For example, a polynomial of the third degree, (its highest exponent is 3), can cross the x-axis at most three times. This rule corresponds to the point made earlier that it can have (at most) three roots. In fact, the graph of a third-degree polynomial can cross *any* horizontal line no more than three times.

⊙ Similarly, for any polynomial, the degree indicates the maximum possible number of times the graph can cross *any* horizontal line.

⊙ Not every polynomial wiggles to the full extent allowed by this law. The polynomial $y = x^5$ crosses each horizontal line just once. But if you can draw a horizontal line that hits the graph four times, then you can be sure that polynomial has a degree of *at least* 4.

In the real world, higher-degree polynomials are actually very important. Some applications of these polynomials include graphic design (used to create esthetically pleasing curves of a variety of shapes), as well as aerodynamic shapes for aircraft, and auto-mobile designs. High-degree polynomials allow the materials to bend smoothly in prescribed ways, which makes them useful for aerodynamics in these industries.

STUDY SIDEKICK

Quiz 6

1. The coefficient for the highest power of x in a higher-degree polynomial is called the _____. The coefficient for the term of a higher-degree polynomial that has no x in it is called the

_____.

2. Multiply $(x - 3)(x^3 + 4x^2 - 2x - 1)$.

3. Use long division to find the roots of
$0 = 3m^3 - 8m^2 + 7m - 2$.

4. The shape of the graph of any polynomial is dictated by its

_____.

5. The constant coefficient of a polynomial is the same as its
____-intercept.

6. The graph of an even polynomial with a negative leading coefficient will open in this direction: _____

7. The graph of an odd polynomial with positive leading coefficient will enter the graph from the _____ and exit from the _____ parts of the coordinate system (looking at it from left to right).

8. The roots of a higher-order polynomial are the places where the graph crosses the ____-axis.

OTHER IMPORTANT STUFF

This section includes some other important stuff relating to material covered in The Adventurous World of College Algebra Parts 1 and 2. Some of this stuff is simply a summary of the video, and some is helpful material we couldn't cover in the video. Read on, campers.

Stuff 1: Algebraic Properties

Here's a nice summary of all the *algebraic* properties for quick and easy reference.

Name	Operation	Property	Check This Out
Closure	Addition	$x + y = z$	Adding two numbers gives you another number.
	Multiplication	$x \cdot y = z$	Multiplying two numbers gives you another number.

STUDY SIDEKICK

Name	Operation	Property	Check This Out
Identity	Addition	$x + 0 = x$	A number doesn't change after addition of 0.
	Multiplication	$x \cdot 1 = x$	A number doesn't change after multiplication by 1.
Associative	Addition	$x + (y + z) = (x + y) + z$	Parentheses around different pairs of numbers is okey-dokey.
	Multiplication	$x(y \cdot z) = (x \cdot y)z$	Parentheses around different pairs of numbers is, too.
Inverse	Addition	$x + (-x) = 0$	Adding a number and its additive inverse equals 0.
	Multiplication	$x \cdot \dfrac{1}{x} = 1$	Multiplying a number and its multiplicative inverse (reciprocal) equals 1.

Name	Operation	Property	Check This Out
Commutative	Addition	$x + y = y + x$	Change in the order of the numbers
	Multiplication	$x \cdot y = y \cdot x$	Change in the order of the numbers
Distributive	Both	$x(y + z) = xy + xz$ $(x + y)z = xz + yz$	Multiplying across parentheses

Stuff 2: Forms of Linear Equations

Here are some excellent reminders about *linear equations*.

The standard form: $Ax + By + C = 0$

The slope-intercept form: $y = mx + b$, where m is the slope and b is the y-intercept

The point-slope form: $y - y_1 = m(x - x_1)$, where m is the slope

A horizontal line: $y = a$, where a is any real number. The x-axis has the equation $y = 0$.

A vertical line: $x = c$, where c is any real number. The y-axis has the equation $x = 0$.

Stuff 3: How to Evaluate an Expression

Here is the basic order for you to follow when *evaluating* an expression.

Step 1: Simplify the expression.

a. Following the order of operations, simplify inside parentheses or other grouping symbols.

b. Simplify exponents.

c. Multiply and divide, working from left to right.

d. Add and subtract, working from left to right, being certain the terms are alike except for the numerical coefficients.

e. Remove parentheses by performing indicated operations and using the distributive property.

f. Combine similar terms.

Step 2: Substitute the indicated numbers (or expressions) for the independent variables.

Stuff 4: How to Solve a Linear Equation

Here's a summary of how to solve a linear equation.
Immediately following Stuff 4, proceed cautiously to Stuff 5.

Step 1: Simplify the left side of the equation.

Step 2: Simplify the right side of the equation.

Step 3: Collect all the variable terms on the left side of the equation and all the constant terms on the right side, using the additive inverses where necessary, or $x + (-x) = 0$.

Step 4: Combine similar terms.

Step 5: Multiply or divide both sides of the equation by the reciprocal (multiplicative inverse) of the numerical coefficient of the variable terms.

Step 6: Check your answers by substitution into the original equation.

Stuff 5. How to Make Instant Coffee

Step 1: Add hot water.

Step 2: Stir.

Step 3: Add Kahlua.

Stuff 6: How to Graph Using a Rectangular Coordinate System

Basically, here you've got all the steps for *graphing* it out in plain English. Super.

Step 1: Draw the axes and label them. Remember, the x-axis is horizontal and the y-axis is vertical.

Step 2: Mark off equal distances on the axes and number them. The intersection of the axes is the origin point $(0,0)$. The positive x-axis points to the right and the positive y-axis points up.

Step 3: Find at least two ordered-pair solutions to the linear equation you want to graph. Easy points to remember and use can be found by first setting $x = 0$ and solving for y and then setting $y = 0$ and solving for x, giving you $(0,y)$ and $(x,0)$.

Step 4: Plot the points. To do this, remember that for each point (x,y), you place your pencil point at the origin, then move x number of units to the right or left (depending on whether x is positive or negative), then move y number of units up or down (depending on whether y is positive or negative). Make a dot at the last place you moved the pencil point to and label it with the (x,y) it represents.

Step 5: Connect the points with a straight line that passes through each point and extends beyond each. Draw small arrowheads at each end to show that the line extends to infinity and label the line with its equation.

Step 6: Pick a point along your line, note its coordinates, and substitute its x and y coordinates into the equation of the line. If you don't get an equality when you finish simplifying, recheck your math. You may have made an arithmetic or drawing error.

Stuff 7: How to Solve Word Problems

Yes, your favorite type of problem, the *word problem*.
If you follow these basic steps, *your* problems will quickly be demystified.

Step 1: Read the problem and decide how many variables there are. Name the variable and write it as "Let $x =$ _____."

Step 2: Translate the words into mathematical equation(s). Here are some useful translations (but always read the problem before and after translating to be sure your equation makes sense):

"equals"   is, was, are

"plus"   increased by, added to, and, more than, sum of

"minus"	decreased by, subtracted from, less than, difference between
"multiply"	product, times, double (or triple)
"divide"	per, reciprocal, quotient

Step 3: Solve the mathematical equation.

Step 4: Check the solution in the original equation.

Step 5: Check the solution against the word problem to be sure it is reasonable and that your translation is correct. If it's not reasonable within the framework of the word problem, it probably isn't right.

Stuff 8: Multiplying Binomials with FOIL

Step 1: Multiply the **F**irst two terms (write this product down).

Step 2: Multiply the **O**uter two terms (write this product down).

Step 3: Multiply the **I**nner two terms (write this product down).

Step 4: Multiply the **L**ast two terms (write this product down).

Step 5: Finally, add or subtract the four terms you found with **FOIL**, combining like terms wherever you can.

Here's an example:

$$\text{Multiply } (x + 3y)(x + 4).$$

Here it is in symbols: **Here it is in words:**

$(x + 3y)(x + 4) = x^2 +$ _____

Multiply the first two terms (write down the product).

$(x + 3y)(x + 4) = x^2 + 4x +$ _____

Multiply the outer two terms (write down the product).

$(x + 3y)(x + 4) = x^2 + 4x + 3xy +$ _____

Multiply the inner two terms (write down the product).

$(x + 3y)(x + 4) = x^2 + 4x + 3xy + 12y$

Multiply the last two terms (write down the product).

Notice that this expansion has no like terms, so we just leave the answer at the fourth step.

Stuff 9: Squaring a Binomial

This is a shortcut for squaring a binomial. You can always use FOIL to check yourself (and you should check yourself every time when you're learning this).

Step 1: Square the first term (and write down the product).

Step 2: Multiply the first and last terms together and then double that (and write down the product). Don't forget the signs of the first and last terms when you do this.

Step 3: Square the last term (and write down the product).

Step 4: Complete the indicated operations, if any, for each new term you have written down. (After not to much practice you can do this in your head as you go along.)

Here's an example. Perform the indicated operation:

$$(x - 3)^2$$

Here it is in symbols:

$$(x - 3)^2 = x^2 + \underline{}$$

Here it is in words:

Square the first term (and write down the product).

Does not include tags, tax and title.

- The guy at the end of the car commercial

202

$(x - 3)^2 = x^2 + [2(x)(-3)] + \underline{\quad}$

Multiply the first and last terms together and then double that (and write down the product).

$(x - 3)^2 = x^2 + [2(x)(-3)] + (-3^2)$

Square the last term (and write down the product).

$(x - 3)^2 = x^2 - 6x + 9$

Complete the indicated operations.

Stuff 10: Factoring Common Polynomials

Here are some more complicated polynomials and shortcuts for factoring them. Enjoy!

Here it is in symbols:

$$(x^2 - y^2) = (x - y)(x + y)$$

Here it is in words:

Every time you see the expression, $(x^2 - y^2)$ you can always factor the expression as $(x - y)(x + y)$. But BE CAREFUL: the sum of two squares $(x^2 + y^2)$ does not factor!

Here it is in symbols:

$$(x^2 + 2xy + y^2) = (x + y)^2$$

Here it is in words:

> Factors of a perfect-square trinomial with a positive middle term equals the sum of the square roots of the first and last terms, quantity squared (BE CAREFUL: make sure you have this exact pattern).

Here it is in symbols:

$$(x^2 - 2xy + y^2) = (x - y)^2$$

Here it is in words:

> Factors of a perfect-square trinomial with a negative middle term equal the difference of the square roots of the first and last terms, quantity squared (BE CAREFUL: make sure you have this exact pattern).

Here it is in symbols:

$$(x^3 + y^3) = (x + y)(x^2 - xy + y^2)$$

Here it is in words:

Factors of the sum of two cubes equal the sum of the cube roots, times the square of the first term minus the product of the first and second term plus the square of the second term (BE CAREFUL: make sure you have this exact pattern).

Here it is in symbols:

$$(x^3 - y^3) = (x - y)(x^2 + xy + y^2)$$

Here it is in words:

Factors of the difference of two cubes are the difference of the cube roots times the square of the first term plus the product of the first and second term plus the square of the second term (BE CAREFUL: make sure you have this exact pattern).

Stuff 11: Useful Formulas

Point-slope equation of a line, used when you know the slope, m, and one point on the line:

$$y - y_1 = m(x - x_1)$$

Slope-intercept equation of a line, used when you know the slope, m, and the y-intercept, b, of a line:

$$y = mx + b$$

Slope of a line, used when you know two points (y_2, y_1) and (x_2, x_1) on a line:

$$m = \frac{y_2 - y_1}{x_1 - x_1}$$

Area of a rectangle, where l is the length and w is the width (or b is the base and h is the height):

$$A = lw \text{ (or, } A = bh)$$

Area of a square, where s is the length of any side:

$$A = s^2$$

Area of a triangle, where b is the base and h is the height:

$$A = \frac{1}{2}bh$$

Area of a circle, where r is the radius (and π is approximately equal to 3.14159):

$$A = \pi r^2$$

Perimeter of a rectangle, where l is the length and w is the width (or b is the base and h is the height):

$$P = 2l + 2w \text{ [or, sometimes, } P = 2b + 2h]$$

Perimeter of a square, where s is the length of any side:

$$P = 4s$$

Perimeter of a triangle, where a, b, and c are the lengths of the sides of the triangle:

$$P = a + b + c$$

Circumference of a circle, where r is the length of the radius:

$$C = 2\pi r$$

Volume of a rectangular solid (box), where l is the length and w is the width (of the base) and h is the height:

$$V = lwh$$

Volume of a square solid, where s is the length of any of the sides:

$$V = s^3$$

Volume of a sphere, where r is the length of the radius:

$$V = \frac{4}{3}\pi r^3$$

Position of a body that is falling down (or rising up), where g is the acceleration of gravity (either 32 feet per second per second OR 9.8 meters per second, depending on whether you are using the English or metric system of measurement); v_0 is the initial velocity (0 when objects are simply dropped); and height is the initial height. If you throw something up, v_0 must be greater than 0. If you throw something down, v_0 must be less than 0.

$$y = \left(\frac{-1}{2}\right)gx^2 + v_0 x + h$$

The quadratic formula, which requires that the equation is solved in the form $ax^2 + bx + c = 0$. No other form is permitted!

$$x = \frac{-b \pm \sqrt{b^2 4ac}}{2a}$$

Nonuseful Formulas:

$$A = a + (\textbf{cucumber})^2 + \frac{1}{4}(\textbf{banana})(\textbf{socks})$$

$A =$ An interesting, healthy, yet not-so-tasty salad

Stuff 12: How to Order Food at

The Varsity Fast Food Restaurant
in Atlanta, Georgia

The Varsity Fast Food Restaurant, located adjacent to the Georgia Tech University campus in midtown Atlanta, is one of the few remaining drive-in fast food restaurants in the country. Yes, the waiters and waitresses actually will set the food right on your car windowsill in the parking lot. Of course, you can walk right inside and order your food at one of the many counters, but you better know what you want…and you better know how to order it!

Ordering Instructions at the Varsity

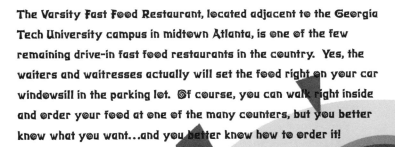

If you want a chili dog, you say:

"I'll have a dog."

If you want a plain hot dog with no chili, you say:

"I'll have a naked dog."

If you want your food to go, you say:

"I'll have it walking."

If you want a plain hot dog to go, you say:

"I'll have a walking, naked dog."

Properly pronounced, that would be "I'll have a walgen, nagid dawg."

Stuff 13: An Example Word Problem

We are about to give you an example word problem of a tricky type of algebra: systems of linear equations. This is merely to whet your appetite for what you will find in The Dangerous World of Pre-Calculus Part 1, which is the next tape in this series. In Pre-Calculus Part 1, we will deal with systems of linear equations in great detail, so check it out.

⊙ Here is an example using a system of linear equations:

> The owners of a 16,000–seat arena sold out the arena for a concert. Floor seats cost $27.50 each, but bleacher seats cost $20.00 each (handling fees were extra, but that's another story so we'll ignore them for this problem). The total gross cash received for the tickets was $331,250.

A. How many tickets were sold for floor seats and bleacher seats?

B. If the owners had decided to charge $45 for floor seats and $40 for bleacher seats, how much would the gross cash receipts be when the arena sold out?

Solution:

⊙ Let x = the number of floor seat tickets sold.

⊙ Let y = the number of bleacher seat tickets sold.

⊙ Then $x + y = 16,000$ the total number of tickets sold.

⊙ And $27.50x + $20.00y = $331,250 ,the gross cash received.

⊙ So the system of equations in this problem is

$$x + y = 16,000$$

$$27.5x + 20y = 331,250$$

⊙ Let's use substitution to solve part A of this problem:

Part One:

Pick a simple equation in the system and solve it for one of the variables. It's your choice, so try to make it easy on yourself.

$$\text{Let } y = 16,000 - x$$

Substitute the solution you just found into the OTHER equation in the system.

$$27.5x + 20(16,000 - x) = 331,250$$

Carry out the indicated operation (using the distributive property).

$$27.5x + 320,000 - 20x = 331,250$$

Collect like terms, keeping the variables on one side of the equation and the constants on the other side.

$$27.5x - 20x = 331,250 - 320,000$$

211

Carry out the indicated operations.

$$7.5x = 11,250$$

Carry out the indicated operations to solve for x.

$$x = \frac{11,250}{7.5}$$

$$x = 1,500$$

Part Two:

Pick the simplest equation in the original system of equations.

We know $x + y = 16,000$.

Substitute the value of x that we just found in Part One of this solution.

$$1,500 + y = 16,000$$

Collect like terms and solve for y.

$$y = 16,000 + 1,500 = 14,500$$

DREADED CHECK

Part Three (the Dreaded Check):

Pick the OTHER equation in the system.

We know $27.5x + 20y = 331,250$.

Substitute both answers we just found in Parts One and Two of this solution.

$$27.5(1,500) + 20(14,500) = 331,250$$

Do the indicated multiplication.

$$41,250 + 290,000 = 331,250$$

Do the indicated addition. Since we have an equality, we're finished if we translated the problem properly.

$$331,250 = 331,250$$

⊙ So, there are 1,500 floor seats and 14,500 bleacher seats in this arena.

On to part **B**:

Now we just want to find the gross receipts for different ticket prices. Since we already know the number of seats, we just rewrite the second equation of the original system as:

$$45(1,500) + 40(14,500) = 67,500 + 580,000 = 647,500$$

The total gross cash receipts for a sold-out arena at the new, higher ticket prices amount to $647,500.

PRACTICE EXAM 3

Using the graph paper at the back of the workbook, graph of the following equations:

1. $y = -2x^2$

2. $y = (x + 2)(x + 3)$

3. $y = x^2 - 1$

4. $y = (x - \sqrt{2})(x + \sqrt{2})$

5. $y = 0.5x^3 + x^2 + 1$

6. A student is standing beneath the window of the room where his girlfriend lives. He agrees to run some errands for her while she studies so they can go out together later on, but he needs her car keys to do so. (Note that the boyfriend in this word problem also likes to cook and clean…and he cried when he saw the movie "The English Patient.")

a. If she drops them to him from her dorm window, which is exactly 36 feet above his outstretched hands, how long will he have between the time she drops the keys and the time he catches them to move his hands into position for the great grab, given that the formula for the distance traveled by a falling body is

$$y = -\frac{1}{2}gx^2 + v_0x + h$$

where $g = 32$ ft/sec^2

The initial velocity is v_0 (in this case, 0, since the keys are simply dropped), h is the initial height of the falling object, and x is time.

b. If she is just a little cross because he interrupted her and she tosses the keys down with a little extra flick of the wrist, so that the initial velocity is 10 feet per second, how much time does her boyfriend have to move his hands into position?

c. If they don't live on the Earth's surface, but are in the same relative positions in a space habitat where g is $\frac{1}{4}$ that of the earth's surface, how much time does her boyfriend have to move his hands into position when she simply drops the keys?

7. A group of students who are taking a short break from their studies have gone outside and are amusing themselves by tossing small stuffed animals straight overhead, timing the period between the toss and the catch, with both toss and catch made at the exact same location, and then calculating the initial velocity for each toss to see who has the best arm.

What is the initial velocity of the small, purple, stuffed animal if it is tossed and caught exactly five seconds later at the same place from which it was tossed?

*** Disclaimer: We at Cerebellum would like to repeat that the objects in this word problem were stuffed, not real animals. Please do not play catch with your neighbor's pets without asking permission. Thank you.

8. Students working on a float for the Homecoming Parade have decided they need to test the brakes of the car being used as a base for the float after both car and float have been fully loaded with props and people. If the braking distance of the car is given approximately by the equation

$$d = v + \left(\frac{v^2}{15}\right)$$

where d is the braking distance (measured in feet) and v is velocity (measured in feet per seconds), how fast can they drive and still have a braking distance less than 25 feet (the distance between their float and the marching band)? Given that 5,280 feet are in a mile and 3,600 seconds in an hour, convert your answer to the first part of this problem to miles per hour.

Bonus: Rework this problem and figure that the car used for the homecoming float is a Yugo. Then the time needed for breaking increases by $10(27^{38})$. Also, assume that the car probably no longer has working brakes. (Just kidding.)

9. As the altitude of a space shuttle increases, the weights of the pilot and passengers decrease until the pilots and passengers become weightless. The weight of a passenger who weighs 145 pounds on Earth is given by:

$$w = 145\left(\frac{6400}{6400 + x}\right)^2$$

where x is the altitude from the surface of the earth and above. At what attitude is the passenger's weight less than 10 pounds?

10. A bottle rocket designed for a science project is shot into the air (under proper supervision) and flies straight up, then straight down again. If its initial velocity is known to have been 40 feet per second, how long was its flight?

11. Instead of studying algebra, a student is dropping bits of turkey for her cat to catch and eat. If she drops the turkey bits from a height of four feet and the cat can catch the turkey when it has dropped two feet, how much time has the cat used to figure out where the turkey will be and then get into position to catch it? How long will it be before the cat tires of this game?

12. Students playing a game of billiards have noticed that they can model the motion of a struck billiard ball, including its bounces off the bumpers of the table. They do this by collecting data on the position of the ball at various times after it was hit. Then the students fit the points into a curve that they recognized as a polynomial. They find that one such curve is given by the equation:

$$f(x) = 1.67x^5 - 2.436x^4 + .016x^2 - 50$$

where x is the time after being struck and $f(x)$ is the position of the ball at time x and the line drawn between the middle side pockets of the table is the x-axis.

Given this, how many times would you expect the ball to cross the line that is parallel to the x-axis and 12 inches closer to the far side of the table than the center line?

13. Multiply the following:

a. $(x + 3)(x - 2)$

b. $(x - 3)(y - 2)$

c. $(x - 3)(x - 3)$

d. $(x + 4)(x + 2)$

e. $(2x - 1)(x + 1)$

f. $(3x - y)(x + 2y)$

g. $(2p - q)(3p - 2q)$

h. $(2m - 3n)(2m + 3q)$

14. Multiply the following:

a. $(x^2)(3xy^4)$

b. $(2p + q)(3r)$

c. $(2x + y)(3r)^2$

d. $(2m + n)^2(3r)$

e. $(2x + y)^3(3p)$

15. Factor the following expressions:

a. $x^2 - 3x + 2$

b. $m^2 + 2m + 1$

c. $x^3 - 8y^3$

d. $144x^2 - 169$

e. $25b^2 + 4$

f. $9 - (x^5 - 3x + \pi)^2$

16. Sketch the graph of the following equations:

a. $y = -x^2$

b. $y = \dfrac{1}{4}x^2$

c. $y = x^2 + 4x + 4$

d. $y = -x^2 + 2x - 1$

e. $y = -x^2 - 2x + 3$

17. Find the roots of the following equations:

a. $(x - 2)^2 = 9$

b. $(m + 1)^2 - 8 = 0$

c. $x^2 - x = 12$

d. $m^2 + 4m + 1 = 0$

e. $p^2 + 6 = 0$

STRESS RELIEF

Section A: Matho Searcho

```
O C S N O U T B O Y O K O
A H P I G L E T B A C O N
N I P I C K L E D E A R S
I T E E F D E L K C I P B
A T L S P O H C K R O P I
M E V I T A T U M M O C R
O R E L A T I O N R W E E
D L G D O T A O K B K B R
I I G O E S D R N N I T A
V N R B O G I E I A F T P
I G E F T N R O I A H L S
D S Q U D E L E R R U D U
E G A S U A S C E S F P C
```

Math Terms and Hang-Over Remedies

AXIS, CARE, CHIN, COFFEE, CONSTANT, CURVE, DEEP SLEEP, DEGREE, DISCRIMINANT, DOMAIN,
DOPE, EXAMS, FREEZING LAKE, GREASY EGGS, INFINITY, KIDS, MEIR, MORE ALCOHOL, POINTSLOPE,
TABASCO SAUCE, TYLENOL, ULNA, WATER, WOKE, Y INTERCEPT

Section B: Matho Crosso

Things found in the mouth and other algebraic terms

CROSS

2. lick with this
8. mmm, these make chocolate taste good
9. they sting when drinking orange juice
12. rise over run
14. smack'em
15. open wide, say ah, and check this out
16. *x* squared has a 2 above it called the--

DOWN

1. the point at which an axis is crossed
3. left from that tasty dip at the party
4. we make holes in teeth
6. next to the molars
7. two terms exactly
8. they give us lovely stinking breath
10. math expressions held togher with an"="
11. spit
13. pairing 1 dependant variable with 1 independant variable

Section C: The Other Matho Searcho

```
M N R L S M U R F E T T E
N A I A I M M S T U S N Q
P M R R T O M P T I H Z U
S O A G D S E R N P L N A
F W O S E C A V A A O E T
U R X B R S E D I E A B I
N E E E Y R I M N L N J O
C D T K S T O M G E O I N
T N R E R N T E P S R Y L
I O E U I I B E I S H B U
O W V B K R K E B T O I C
N O T R A D I C A L U N Y
S Q U A R E E C G R A P H
```

Math Terms and Famous Female Cartoon Stars

ALGEBRA, BENZ, BETTY BOOP, BINOMIAL, BRENDA STARR, CATHY, DAPHNE, DART, EQUATION, FUNCTION, GRAPH, INTERCEPT, INVERSE, JOSIE, KIRK, KURD, LINEAR, LUCY, MARGE SIMPSON, MIRA, MODS, OLIVE OIL, OPTS, RADICAL, SMURFETTE, SQUARE, STUS, VERTEX, WONDER WOMAN

Section D: The Other Matho Crosso

Math Terms and T.V. Trivia

ACROSS

2. most popular show on TNN
8. Fonzie's first name
9. "Dukes of Hazzard" U.S. Congressman
13. y 5 x squared, St. Louis Arch, & big belly
16. Jack Tripper's profession
17. not on Pamela Anderson
18. Clinton, Reagan, and this have two terms
20. no one admits they have one
22. "My _____ Sons"
24. Conan O'Brien wrote for this show

DOWN

1. Greg Brady's rock star persona
3. "Eight is Enough" city
4. math term & what you attempt to do in the AM
5. Willis on Different Strokes had this problem
6. this TV mogul's daughter is a 90210 star
7. word for exponent and Bill Gates
10. four-sided figure and a geek
11. <, #, %, and a percussion instrument
12. Tattoo couldn't have this on "Fantasy Island"
14. City where "Homicide" is filmed
15. this show switched "Darrens" midseason
16. math deity's gift to students
19. tooth fairy, Santa, nice guys & girls
21. B.J.'s first name on "M.A.S.H."
23. equations, dyed hair, & trees have these

DALE GOES TO DENTAL SCHOOL

by Dr. Dale Ungulate (Giraffe)

Go ahead and make fun all you want, I've heard them all…"Hey, don't hit your head walking under that bridge," or how about, "Yo, nice horns, hoof boy," to which I politely reply, "They're not horns, they are bony protuberances called ossicones, thank you very much." It's not so easy being a giraffe in today's world, which is why my mother almost lost her spots when I told her I wanted to leave the zoo to become a dentist. I don't think there is a dentist alive who could

verbally explain to you why he or she wanted to become a dentist. All I can say is that it's best described as a calling, an internal desire if you will, to not just understand teeth, but to vicariously live through them and feel their pain and needs. I love the practice of dental medicine, and I call myself a dentist with a sense of pride and reverence. Are there some down sides? Sure, what profession doesn't? If I had an acacia leaf for every time someone has come up to me and said, "Hey doc, check out my gums. How bout' that smile, baby!" I would surely be one chubby giraffe. As if I would bring my kitchen sink to the restaurant where my plumber was dining with his family and say, "Hey, aren't my pipes rust–free?"

Pardon me for venting; I digress. Anyway, I had pretty decent grades in school and I studied hard. Yeah, like most college students I partied hard and hooked up a lot (my parents weren't so thrilled to hear that I was dating humans; Mom's best

illustration by: Holly Black

227

friend had a gazelle she wanted me to meet) but I was diligent in my pursuit of the dental sciences. When I applied to dental school, I "accidentally" forgot to mark "giraffe" under the "other" category. So, naturally, I was accepted, and on my first day I encountered quite a few stares. The insults were harsh, but I held back the tears. I spent a fortune on specially designed dental instruments to accommodate my hooves, and I had to practically beg on two legs for the administration to plant an acacia tree on the quad to provide for my dining needs. Yes, my neck was put through hell leaning over the examination chair, and I'll never forget the signs posted on my tail which read "Make me talk," but I survived.

Yes, I survived all four years and I'll never forget (even though that's an elephant thing) that blessed day when I said those four magical words…"Spit into the bowl." Yes, I had become a dentist…and a damn good one. Today I have my own practice in the suburbs, I did eventually meet, fall in love with, and marry that gazelle, and my license plate proudly reads "Dr. Hoof."

Thank you for hearing my story.

Dr. Dale Ungulate, D.D.S

THE ANSWERS

Quiz 1 Solutions

1. A function is a relation in which each element of a set is paired with **one and only one** element of the second set.

2. A short way to write "the function of x" is $f(x)$.

3. The standard form for expressing a function is $y = f(x) = ax + b$ or $y = ax + b$, **where a and b are any real numbers.**

4. A "term" in mathematics has two parts, the **constant** and the **variable**.

5. Any math expression or function containing one or more terms is called a **polynomial**.

Quiz 2 Solutions

1. The domain of a function is the set of all values used by the **independent** variable (which is often called x).

2. The range of a function is the set of all values used by the **dependent** variable (which is often called $f(x)$ or y).

3. A function may pair an element of its domain with **one and only one** element of its range.

4. A function may pair an element of its range with **one or more** element(s) of its domain.

5. The horizontal axis of a graph represents values for the **independent (or x) variable**.

6. The range of a function is graphed on the **vertical** axis of a graph.

7. If an equation is graphed and the vertical line test shows that the graph of the equation is touched by the line **one and only one time**, no matter where you apply the test, then the equation is a function.

8. Inverting a graph means that you reverse the coordinates of each point on the graph, so the points (0, 3), (2, 26), and (−0.002, 13) would become **(3, 0)**, **(26, 2)**, and **(13, −0.002)**.

9. If $f(x) = 6x + 10$, what is its inverse function?

Solving this the short way, we exchange x and $f(x)$, renaming $f(x)$ as $g(x)$:

$$x = 6g(x) + 10$$

then use the algebraic properties to put the equation in standard form:

$$-6g(x) = -x + 10$$

$$g(x) = \frac{x}{6} - \frac{10}{6}$$

and then simplify:

$$g(x) = \frac{x}{6} - \frac{5}{3}$$

And now we check. Let $x = 1$. Plug it into the original equation. Then $f(1) = 6(1) + 10 = 16$. Now, plug 16 into the $g(x)$ equation: $g(16) = \frac{16}{6} - \frac{5}{3} = \frac{8-5}{3} = \frac{3}{3} = 1$, exactly what we started with!

10. What is the inverse function of $f(x) = \frac{3x}{2} - \frac{2}{5}$?

Solving this the short way, we exchange x and $f(x)$, renaming $f(x)$ as $g(x)$:

$$x = \frac{3g(x)}{2} - \frac{2}{5}$$

and then use the algebraic properties to put the equation in standard form: (remember to multiply by sides of the equation when manipulating!)

$$10x = 15g(x) - 4$$

$$-15g(x) = -10x - 4$$

$$g(x) = \frac{-10x - 4}{-15}$$

$$g(x) = \frac{10x + 4}{15}$$

Once again, we check using a simple (easy to calculate with) number for x, such as (ahem) 1:

$$f(1) = \frac{3(1)}{2} - \frac{2}{5} = \frac{15 - 4}{10} = \frac{11}{10}$$

Now plug $11/10$ into $g(x)$

$$g(11/10) = \frac{10(11/10) + 4}{15} = \frac{11 + 4}{15} = \frac{15}{15} = 1$$

So your inverse function was correct!

Quiz 3 Solutions

1. Match the algebraic property with the equation shown below:

A. __6__ $x(yz) = (xy)z$ 1. Additive property

B. __3__ $x + y = y + x$ 2. Associative property
                                                  for addition

C. __5__ $x(y + z) = xy + xz$ 3. Commutative prop-
                                                  erty for addition

D. __8__ $x \cdot 1 = x$ 4. Additive property

E. __7__ $xy = yx$

5. Distributive property

F. __4__ $x + (-x) = 0$

6. Associative property for multiplication

G. __9__ $x \cdot \dfrac{1}{x} = 1$

7. Commutative property for multiplication

H. __1__ $x + 0 = x$

8. Multiplicative identity property

I. __2__ $x + (y + z) = (x + y) + z$

9. Multiplicative property

2. The slope of a line is the **rate of change** between two points and is commonly thought of as the ratio of the **rise over the run**. Its symbol is *m*.

3. Find the slope and *y*-intercept of the following equations:

   a. $y = .65x + 4$

Because this equation is clever enough to be in the point-slope form (where $y = mx + b$), we know just by looking at it that its slope is .65 and its *y*-intercept is 4.

   b. $f(x) = 3 - 2x$

This equation is almost in the point-slope form.
Let's rewrite it as:

$$f(x) = -2x + 3$$

so we read off the slope as -2 and the $y-$intercept as 3.

4. Using the point-slope form, you can find the equation of a line with **two** point(s).

5. Find the equation of the line, given:

a. $(-4, 0)$ and $(0, -2)$

For this, we use the point-slope form of a line, letting (x_1, y_1) be $(-4, 0)$ and (x_2, y_2) be $(0, -2)$, and first find the slope like so:

$$m = \frac{y_2 - y_1}{x_2 - x_1} = \frac{-2 - 0}{0 - (-4)} = \frac{-2}{4} = \frac{-1}{2}$$

Pretty easy so far. Now we just substitute into the point-slope form:

$$y - y_1 = m(x - x_1)$$

$$y - 0 = \frac{-1}{2}[x - (-4)]$$

and use the algebraic properties to neaten up the equation:

$$y = \frac{-x - 4}{2}$$

$$y = \frac{-x}{2} - 2$$

Checking, we just substitute x_2 for x and see if we get y_2:

$$y = \frac{-0}{2} - 2 = -2$$

so we're done and we know we're correct. Yeah!

b. (3, 6) and y−intercept = 2

This one looks a little ugly, but it isn't. Remembering that the y-intercept is just the point where the line crosses the y-axis, we know that the value for x must be 0. So we really have two points again, (3, 6) and (0, 2), and we proceed just as in problem 5a.

For this, we use the point-slope form of a line, this time letting (x_1, y_1) be (3, 6) and (x_2, y_2) be (0, 2), and first finding the slope like so:

$$m = \frac{y_2 - y_1}{x_2 - x_1} = \frac{2 - 6}{0 - 3} = \frac{-4}{-3} = \frac{4}{3}$$

Just as easy as before. Now we just substitute into the point-slope form:

$$y - y_1 = m(x - x_1)$$

$$y - 6 = \frac{4}{3}(x - 3)$$

and use the algebraic properties to neaten up the equation:

$$y = \frac{4x}{3} - \frac{4(3)}{3} + 6$$

$$y = \frac{4x}{3} + 2$$

Checking, we just substitute x_2 for x and see if we get y_2:

$$y = \frac{4(0)}{3} + 2 = 0 + 2 = 2$$

So we're done and we know we're correct.

6. Find the equation of a line parallel to $3x + y = 6$.

To solve this, we must recall that parallel lines have the same slope and different y-intercepts. Then, since we can directly find the slope and y-intercept of an equation in standard form, we first put this equation in standard form:

$$y = -3x + 6$$

Now, to find a parallel line we can pick any number except 6 for the y-intercept. So $y = -3x + 0$ is correct, $y = -3x + 1$ is correct, and $y = -3x - 2.5$ is correct. All of these lines and, in fact, an infinite number of lines whose equations have the form $y = -3x + c$, where c is any real number except 6, are parallel to $3x + y = 6$. Done.

7. Find the slope of a line perpendicular to $3x + y = 6$.

For this problem, we have to recall that the slopes of perpendicular lines are negative inverses of each other. Once again, we put the equation in standard form: $y = -3x + 6$. Then you can write the general equation of the perpendicular line as $y = \frac{1(x)}{3} + c$, where c is any real number you want to pick.

8. A function's root is its x-intercept.

9. Find the root of $x + 2y = 14$.

To find the root of a linear equation, we remember that it is the same as the x-intercept. Then we recall that the x-intercept has a value for y of 0. Now that we know y, we just substitute into the equation, like so:

$$x + 2(0) = 14$$

and use the algebraic properties to solve the equation for x:

$$x + 0 = 14$$

$$x = 14$$

And that's all there is to it.

10. The number of roots in a polynomial equation is equal to the **order or degree** of the equation.

Quiz 4 Solutions

1. A square root can be written in two different ways. So, the square root of thirteen can be written as $13^{1/2}$ or $\sqrt{13}$.

2. What are the square roots of 1, 121, 4, 100, 9, 81, 16, 64, 25, 49, 36?

They are, in the same order: 1, 11, 2, 10, 3, 9, 4, 8, 5, 7, 6.

3. A binomial has **exactly two** term(s).

4. What is:

a. $(6x)^2$?

$$(6x)^2 = (6x)(6x) = \mathbf{36x^2}$$

b. $(4x - 3)^2$?

$$(4x - 3)^2 = (4x - 3)(4x - 3)$$

$$= (4x)(4x) + (4x)(-3) + (-3)(4x) + (-3)(-3)$$

$$= 16x^2 - 12x - 12x + 9$$

$$= \mathbf{16x^2 - 24x + 9}$$

5. a. What does FOIL stand for?

First terms, Outer terms, Inner terms, Last terms

b. When is it used?

It is used when multiplying two binomials.

6. Which of the following are in the standard form of a quadratic equation?

a. $y = 3x - 12$

This is a linear equation (its order is 1), so it is **not** in the standard form of a quadratic equation.

b. $4x^2 + y - 13 = 0$

This **is** a quadratic equation, but it is **not** in standard form because all the variables are on the same side of the equal sign.

c. $y = (x + 1)(2x - 7)$

This is a quadratic equation, but it is **not** in standard form because the indicated multiplication has not been carried out and simplified.

d. $y = 3^{1/2} x^2 + 4x - 5$

This **is** a quadratic equation in standard form.

7. When graphed, a quadratic equation takes the form of a **parabola**.

8. A vertical line drawn through the vertex of the graph of a quadratic equation is called its **axis of symmetry**.

9. Given $y = ax^2 + bx + c$,

   a. What is the y–intercept of the parabola?

   The y–intercept is c, located at (0, c).

   b. What is the equation for the axis of symmetry of the parabola?

   $$x = \frac{-b}{2a}$$

10. Given $y = 4x^2 + 4x + 1$,

   a. What is the y–intercept?

   1

   b. What is the axis of symmetry?

   $$x = \frac{-b}{2a}$$

   $$x = \frac{-4}{(2)(4)}$$

   $$x = \frac{-1}{2}$$

c. Where is the vertex of this parabola?

We know that $x = \frac{-1}{2} = -0.5$, so we plug this value for x into the equation to find the y value, like so:

$$y = 4x^2 + 4x + 1$$

$$y = 4(-0.5)^2 + 4(-0.5) + 1$$

$$y = 1 - 2 + 1$$

$$y = 0$$

So the vertex is at $(-0.5, 0)$.

Quiz 5 Solutions

1. A quadratic equation may have a maximum of **two** real root(s), which is where the graph of the equation touches the $x-$**axis**.

2. When you break a quadratic equation down into the product of two binomials, you are **factoring** it.

3. Find the factors of $x^2 + x - 12$.

$$x^2 + x - 12 = (x + 4)(x - 3)$$

4. If a factor of an equation is $(x - r)$, then a root of the same equation is r.

5. Find the roots of $3x^2 + 7x + 4 = 0$.

$$3x^2 + 7x + 4 = (3x + 4)(x + 1)$$

$$(3x + 4)(x + 1) = 0$$

If $3x + 4 = 0$, $x = \dfrac{-4}{3}$

If $x + 1 = 0$, $x = -1$

So the roots are $\dfrac{-4}{3}$ and -1.

6. Find the roots of $x^2 - 22x = -121$ by factoring.

$$x^2 - 22x = -121, \text{ so}$$

$$x^2 - 22x + 121 = 0$$

$$(x - 11)(x - 11) = 0, \text{ so}$$

$$x = 11$$

There is only one real root of this quadratic: 11.

7. Given $4x^2 + 20x + 25$,

a. The name of this expression is *perfect square trinomial*.

b. The factors of this expression are **$(2x + 5)(2x + 5)$**.

8. Find the roots of $4x^2 + 20x + 36 = 11$.

$4x^2 + 20x + 36 = 11$ means $4x^2 + 20x + 25 = 0$.

So, $(2x + 5)(2x + 5) = 0$

And $x = \frac{-5}{2}$. **There is only one real root.**

9. Given $144 - 49x^2$.

a. The name of this expression is **the difference of two squares**.

b. The factors of this expression are $(12 + 7x)(12 - 7x)$.

10. The quadratic formula can be used for all quadratic equations after they have been put into **standard** form, which is $y = ax^2 + bx + c$.

11. Given $y = x^2 - 3x + 1$, use the quadratic formula to find its root(s).

$y = x^2 - 3x + 1$, so $a = 1$, $b = -3$, and $c = 1$

The discriminant is $b^2 - 4ac = (-3)^2 - 4(1)(1) = 9 - 4 = 5$

so $x = \dfrac{-b \pm \sqrt{b^2 - 4ac}}{2a} = \dfrac{-(-3) \pm \sqrt{5}}{2(1)} = \dfrac{3 \pm \sqrt{5}}{2}$

and the roots are $x = \dfrac{3 + \sqrt{5}}{2}$ and $x = \dfrac{3 - \sqrt{5}}{2}$.

12. An imaginary number is represented by the symbol *i*, which is defined as $\sqrt{-1}$.

13. A complex number is a combination of **real** and **imaginary** numbers.

14. Given $y = x^2 + 3x + 3$, use the quadratic formula to find its root(s).

$y = x^2 - 3x + 3$, so $a = 1$, $b = -3$ and $c = 3$

The discriminant is

$$b^2 - 4ac = (-3)^2 - 4(1)(3) = 9 - 12 = -3$$

so $x = \dfrac{-b \pm \sqrt{b^2 - 4ac}}{2a} = \dfrac{-(-3) \pm \sqrt{-3}}{2(1)} = \dfrac{3 \pm i\sqrt{3}}{2}$

and the roots are $x = \dfrac{3 + i\sqrt{3}}{2}$ and $x = \dfrac{3 - i\sqrt{3}}{2}$.

15. a. Is $y = ax^2 + bx + c$ a quadratic? Is it a function?

It is a quadratic and it is a function, because it is a polynomial of order 2 and there is one and only one y value for each x value for which it is defined.

b. Is $x = ay^2 + by + c$ a quadratic? Is it a function?

It is a quadratic and it is not a function because it is a polynomial of order 2 and there are two possible y values for each x value for which it is defined.

Quiz 6 Solutions

1. The coefficient for the highest power of x in a higher-degree polynomial is called the **leading coefficient**. The coefficient for the term of a higher-degree polynomial that has no x in it is called the **constant coefficient**.

2. Multiply $(x - 3)(x^3 + 4x^2 - 2x - 1)$.

$$(x - 3)(x^3 + 4x^2 - 2x - 1) = (x)(x^3) + (x)(4x^2) + (x)(-2x) + (x)(-1) + (-3)(x^3) + (-3)(4x^2) + (-3)(-2x) + (-3)(-1)$$

$$= x^4 + 4x^3 + (-2x^2) + (-1x) + (-3x^3) + (-12x^2) + 6x + 3$$

$$= x^4 + x^3 - 14x^2 + 5x + 3$$

3. Use long division to find the roots of

$$0 = 3m^3 - 8m^2 + 7m - 2.$$

Let's try $(m - 1)$ first. It's good to start with a simple, small numbers and we know 1 is a factor of -2.

$$
\begin{array}{r}
3m^2 - 5m + 2 \\
m - 1 \overline{)3m^3 - 8m^2 + 7m - 2} \\
\underline{3m^3 - 3m^2} \\
-5m^2 + 7m \\
\underline{-5m^2 + 5m} \\
2m - 2 \\
\underline{2m - 2} \\
0
\end{array}
$$

4. The shape of the graph of any polynomial is dictated by its **degree (or order).**

5. The constant coefficient of a polynomial is the same as its *y*-**intercept**.

6. The graph of an even polynomial with a negative leading coefficient will open in this direction: **downward.**

7. The graph of an odd polynomial with positive leading coefficient will enter the graph from the **bottom left** and exit from the **top right** parts of the coordinate system (looking at it from left to right).

8. The roots of a higher-order polynomial are the places where the graph crosses the *x*-**axis**.

Answers to Practice Exam 1

1. Below are the graph and table values.

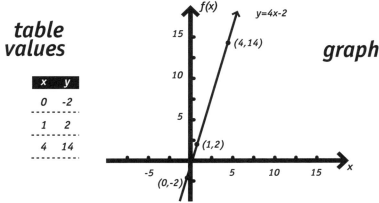

table values

x	y
0	-2
1	2
4	14

graph

2. $y + 1 = x + 3(x - 1)$

$y + 1 = x + 3x - 3$

Graph and table values for $y = 4x - 4$:

table values

x	y
0	-4
1	0
4	12

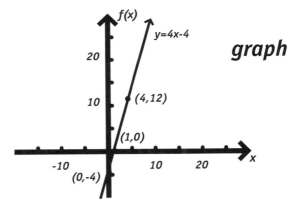

graph

STANDARD DEVIANTS

3. $6x - 24y = 36$

$x - 4y = 6$

Graph and table values for $x = 6 + 4y$:

table values

x	y
6	0
-2	-2
10	1

graph

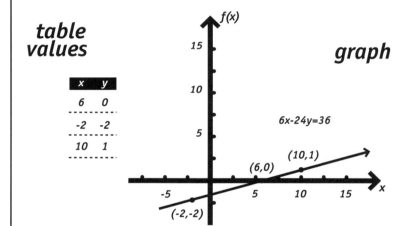

4. $2x = 8$

Graph and table values for $x = 4$:

table values

x	y
4	0
4	-5
4	5

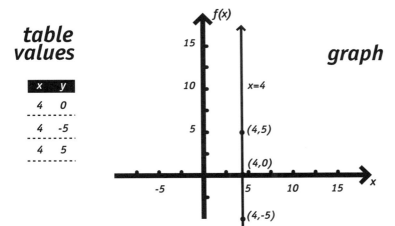

graph

5. Graph and table values for $y = 1$:

table values

x	y
-3	1
0	1
10	1

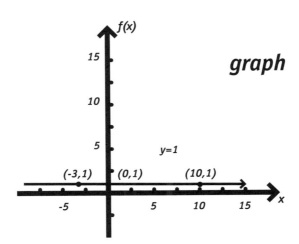

graph

6. Let *l* be the length of one side.

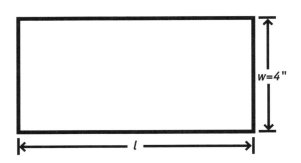

Let *w* be the width of one side.

$$l = 3w$$

Let *P* be the perimeter of the box.

$$P = l + l + w + w$$

$$= 2l + 2w$$

$$= 2(3w) + 2w$$

$$= 6w + 2w$$

$$= 8w$$

Since $w = 4$ inches, $P = (8)(4") = 32"$.

The box has a perimeter of 32".

7. Let the age (now) of one cousin be c_1.

Then, $c_1 + 7 = 3(25)$

$$c_1 + 7 = 75$$

$$c_1 = 75 - 7 = 68$$

One cousin is 68 years old when the student is 18.

Let the age (now) of the second cousin be c_2.

$$c_2 + 4 = \frac{1}{2}(18+4)$$

$$c_2 + 4 = \frac{1}{2}(22)$$

$$c_2 + 4 = 11$$

$$c_2 = 11 - 4$$

$$c_2 = 7$$

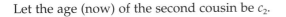

The second cousin is 7 years old when the student is 18.

8. The coffee fills the cup at a rate of $\frac{1}{30}$ per second while the *faux* cream fills the cup at a rate of $\frac{1}{75}$ per second. Let x be the time the cup fills with both coffee and cream.

Then:

$$\frac{1}{30} + \frac{1}{75} = \frac{1}{x}$$

$$150x\left(\frac{1}{30} + \frac{1}{75}\right) = 150x\left(\frac{1}{x}\right)$$

[The lowest common denominator is $150x$.]

$$5x + 2x = 150$$

$$x = \frac{150}{7}$$

$$x = 21\frac{3}{7}$$

The cup will fill with the mixed coffee and cream in $21\frac{3}{7}$ seconds.

Now, if there is a hole, it will allow the fluid in the cup to drain at the rate of $\frac{1}{120}$ per second, so the new equation under these conditions is:

$$\frac{1}{30} + \frac{1}{75} - \frac{1}{120} = \frac{1}{x}$$

$$600x\left(\frac{1}{30} + \frac{1}{75} - \frac{1}{120}\right) = 600x\left(\frac{1}{x}\right)$$

[The lowest common denominator is $600x$.]

$$20x + 8x - 5x + 600$$

$$(20 + 8 - 5)x = 600$$

$$23x = 600$$

$$x = \frac{600}{23}$$

$$x = 26\frac{2}{23} \text{ seconds}$$

With the small hole, it takes $26\frac{2}{3}$ seconds for the cup to fill.

9. a. $5 - 3(4 - 6) = 5 - (3)(-2)$

$$= 5 - (-6)$$

$$= 5 + 6$$

$$= 11$$

b. $-(5 - 4) - (-7 - 6) = -(1) - (-13)$

$= -1 + 13$

$= 12$

10. a. Additive identity property

b. Distributive property

c. Commutative property of multiplication

d. Commutative property of addition

11. a. $3(4x + 2) = (3)(4x) + (3)(2)$ **distributive property**

$= 12x + 6$ **closure property**

$= 6(2x + 1)$ **distributive property**

b. $6(x - 4) + 3(2x + 5)$

$= 6x - (6)(4) + (3)(2x) + (3)(5)$ **distributive property**

$= 6x - 24 + 6x + 15$ **closure**

$= 6x + 6x - 24 + 15$ **collect like terms**

$= (6 + 6)x - 9$ **distributive, closure property**

$= 12x - 9$ **closure property**

$= 3(4x - 3)$ **distributive property**

c. $(y^2 + 35y - 15) + 2(x^2 - y^2 - 16y + 5)$

$= y^2 + 35y - 15 + 2x^2 - 2y^2 - 32y + 10$ **distributive property**

$= y^2 - 2y^2 + 35y - 32y + 2x^2 - 15 + 10$ **collect like terms**

$= (1 - 2)y^2 + (35 - 32)y + 2x^2 + (-15 + 10)$ **distributive property**

$= -y^2 + 3y + 2x^2 - 5$ **closure**

255

Action is

eloquence.

-Aristotle

12. a. $f(x) = 3x + 12$

At $x = 1$, $f(1) = 3(1) + 12$

$= 3 + 12$

$= \mathbf{15}$

b. $g(x) = 5(1 - 6x) = 5 - 30x$

At $x = 3$, $g(3) = 5 - 30(3)$

$= 5 - 90$

$= \mathbf{-85}$

c. $p(y) = 6y + 2(-3 + y) - 4y$

$= 6y - 6 + 2y - 4y$

$= 6y + 2y - 4y - 6$

$= (6 + 2 - 4)y - 6$

so, $p(y) = 4y - 6$

At $y = 2$, $p(2) = 4(2) - 6 = 8 - 6 = 2$

13. a. $3x - 4 - (2x + 6) = 3 - x - 7$

$$3x - 4 - 2x - 6 = 3 - x - 7$$

$$x - 10 = -x - 4$$

Add 10 to both sides:

$$x - 10 + 10 = -x - 4 + 10$$

$$x = -x + 6$$

Add x to both sides:

$$x + x = -x + x + 6$$

$$2x = 6$$

Multiply both sides by $\frac{1}{2}$:

$$\frac{1}{2}(2x) = \frac{1}{2}(6)$$

$$x = 3$$

Check your answer:

$$3(3) - 4 - [(2)(3) + 6] = 3 - 3 - 7$$

$$9 - 4 - 12 = 3 - 10$$

$$9 - 16 = -7$$

$$-7 \cong -7$$

b. $4(2y + 5) - 3(y - 6) = 18$

$$8y + 20 - 3y + 18 = 18$$

$$5y + 38 = 18$$

Add -38 to both sides:

$$5y + 38 - 38 = 18 - 38$$

$$5y = -20$$

Multiply both sides by $\frac{1}{5}$:

$$\frac{1}{5}(5y) = \frac{1}{5}(-20)$$

$$y = -4$$

Check your answer:

$$4[(2)(-4) + 5] - 3(-4 - 6) = 18$$

$$4[-8 + 5] - 3(-10) = 18$$

$$4(-3) + 30 = 18$$

$$-12 + 30 = 18$$

$$18 \cong 18$$

c. $2x + 3x(1 + 3) + 4(x + 3) = 2$

$$2x + 3x(4) + 4(x + 3) = 2$$

$$2x + 12x + 4x + 12 = 2$$

$$18x + 12 = 2$$

STANDARD DEVIANTS

Add -12 to both sides:

$$18x + 12 - 12 = 2 - 12$$

$$18x = -10$$

Multiply both sides by $\dfrac{1}{18}$:

$$\frac{1}{18}(18x) = \frac{1}{18}(-10)$$

$$x = -\frac{10}{18}$$

$$x = -\frac{5}{9}$$

Check your answer:

$$2\left(\frac{-5}{9}\right) + (3)\left(\frac{-5}{9}\right)(1 + 3) + 4\left(\frac{-5}{9} + 3\right) = 2$$

$$\frac{-10}{9} + \left(\frac{-15}{9}\right)(4) + 4\left(\frac{22}{9}\right) = 2$$

$$-\frac{10}{9} - \frac{60}{9} + \frac{88}{9} = 2$$

$$\frac{-10 - 60 + 88}{9} = 2$$

$$\frac{18}{9} = 2$$

$$2 \cong 2$$

Answers to Practice Exam 2

1. a. $\quad 3[(-2)(6) + 4(-5 + 3 - 7)] = 3[(-2)(6) + 4(-9)]$

$\qquad = 3[-12 - 36]$

$\qquad = 3[-48]$

$\qquad = -144$

b. $\dfrac{5^2 - 2}{[(-2)(-3) - 3]}$

$\qquad = \dfrac{25 - 2}{[(-2)(-3) - 3]}$

$\qquad = \dfrac{25 - 2}{6 - 3}$

$\qquad = \dfrac{23}{3} \text{ or } 7\dfrac{2}{3}$

2. a. Multiplicative identity property

b. Closure property

c. Associative property of multiplication

d. Associative property of addition

3. a. $f(x) = 3(4x + 2) = 12x + 6$

at $x = 5$:

$$f(x) = 12(5) + 6$$

$$= 60 + 6$$

$$= 66$$

b. $g(x) = 6(x - 4) + 3(2x + 5)$

$$= 6x - 24 + 6x + 15$$

$$= 12x - 9$$

at $x = 4$,

$g(4) = 12(4) - 9$

$$= 48 - 9$$

$$= 39$$

c. $f(x) = 2(x^2 - 16x + 5)$

$$= 2x^2 - 32x + 10$$

at $x = 2$,

$$f(2) = 2(2)^2 - 32(2) + 10$$

$$= (2)(2)(2) - 64 + 10$$

$$= 8 - 64 + 10$$

$$= -46$$

4. We see that each of these problems has a point and a slope, so we use the point–slope form of a linear equation, $y - y_1 = m(x - x_1)$, to solve them:

a. $m = 2$, $x_1 = 4$, $y_1 = 2$; so, substituting:

$$y - 2 = 2(x - 4)$$

$$y - 2 = 2x - 8$$

$$y = 2x - 6$$

b. $m = 0$, $x_1 = 3$, $y_1 = 1$; so, substituting:

$$y - 1 = 0(x - 3)$$

$$y - 1 = 0$$

$$y = 1$$

c. $m = -1$, $x_1 = 2$, $y_1 = 3$; so, substituting:

$$y - 3 = -1(x - 2)$$

$$y - 3 = -x + 2$$

$$y = -x + 5$$

5. a. Graph and table values for $2x + 3y = 4$

table values

x	y
0	$4/3$
2	0
1	$2/3$

graph

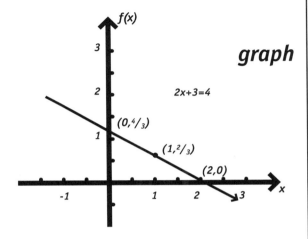

b. Graph and table values for $3x + y = 0$

table values

x	y
0	0
1	-3
-1	3

graph

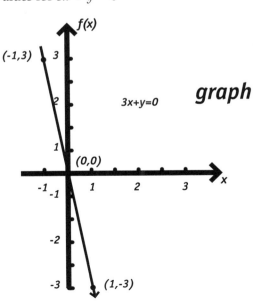

STANDARD DEVIANTS

c. $y + 4 = 5$

$\quad y = 1$

We recognize this as the equation of a horizontal line.

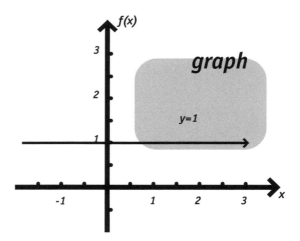

d. $x + 3 = 2$

$x = -1$

We recognize this as the equation of a vertical line.

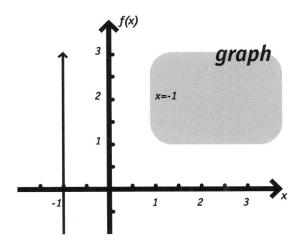

Answers to Practice Exam 3

1. Here is the graph and table of values for $y = -2x^2$:

table values

x	y
0	0
-½	-½
-½	-½
1	-2
-1	-2
2	-8
-2	-8

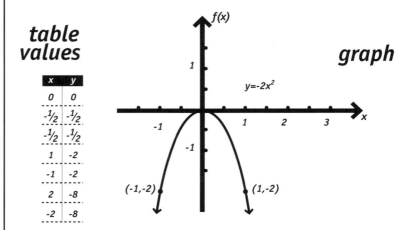

2. Here is the graph and table of values for

$$y = (x - 2)(x - 3) = x^2 - 3x - 2x + 6 = x^2 - 5x + 6:$$

table values

x	y
0	6
-1	12
1	2
2	0
3	0
4	2
5	6

3. Here is the graph and table of values for $y = x^2 - 1$:

table values

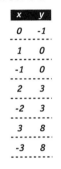

x	y
0	-1
1	0
-1	0
2	3
-2	3
3	8
-3	8

graph

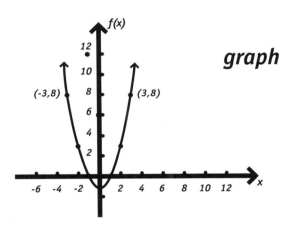

4. Here is the graph and table of values for

$$y = \left(x - \sqrt{2}\right)\left(x + \sqrt{2}\right) = x^2 - 2:$$

table values

x	y
0	-2
1	-1
-1	-1
2	2
-2	2
3	7
-3	7

graph

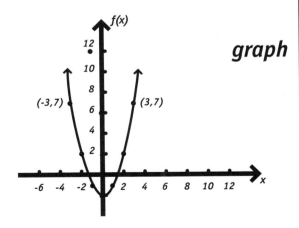

269

5. Here is the graph and table of values for $y = 0.5x^3 + x^2 - 1$:

table values

x	y
0	-1
1	0.5
-1	-0.5
2	7
-2	-1

graph

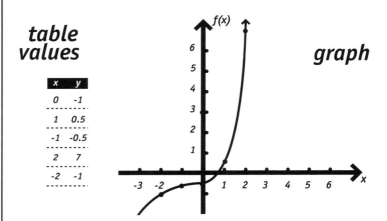

6. a. We know that vertical motion is modeled by $y = -\frac{1}{2} gx^2 + v_0 x + h$, where g is the acceleration of gravity, v_0 is the initial velocity of the falling (or rising) object, h is the initial height of the falling (or rising) object, and x is the time.

For this part of the problem, we let the height at which the keys are caught, or y, be 0, so h is $0 + 36 = 36$ feet. The keys are simply dropped, so the initial velocity is 0. Since we are working with the British system of measurements (feet instead of meters), $g = 32$ feet per second per second.

Substituting these values into the formula, we have $0 = \left(-\frac{1}{2}\right)(32)x^2 + 0x + 36$; and, simplifying, we have $0 = -16x^2 + 36$. Collecting like terms on each side of the equals sign, we have $16x^2 = 36$, so $x^2 = \frac{36}{16} = \frac{9}{4}$. Taking the square root of each side gives us $x = +\frac{3}{2}$ and $-\frac{3}{2}$. Because the keys were dropped at time zero, represented by $x = 0$, and time does not go backward, we can only use the positive root in this problem, so the student has 1.5 seconds to move his hands to catch the keys.

b. The only part of the problem that has changed is the initial velocity, which is now -10 feet per second (since they were tossed down), so we can use the same equation with the new value for v_0, like this:

$$0 = \left(-\frac{1}{2}\right)(32)x^2 - 10x + 36,$$

so $0 = -16x^2 - 10x + 36$, so $16x^2 + 10x - 36 = 0$.

This equation is now in standard form (which is $ax^2 + bx + c = 0$), so we can solve it using the quadratic formula, as follows:

First, the discriminant:

$$b^2 - 4ac = 16^2 - 4(10)(-36) = 256 + 1440 = 1696$$

Now, the quadratic formula:

$$x = \frac{-b \pm \sqrt{b^2 - 4ac}}{2a}$$

$$= \frac{-16 \pm \sqrt{1696}}{2(10)}$$

$$= \frac{-16 \pm 4\sqrt{106}}{20}$$

$$= \frac{-4 \pm \sqrt{106}}{5}$$

With a calculator, we find that $x \approx 1.26$ and $x \approx -2.86$. Once again, since the keys were tossed at $x = 0$, we can only use the positive root in this problem, so the student now has only 1.26 seconds to move his hands into position.

c. In this part, we have to change the value of g from 32 ft/sec^2 to (32/4) or 8 ft/sec^2. Otherwise, the problem is the same as in part A, so we can say:

$$0 = \left(-\frac{1}{2}\right)(8)x^2 + 36 = -4x^2 + 36, \text{ so } 4x^2 = 36.$$

Dividing both sides by 4, we have $x^2 = 9$, so $x = \pm 3$.

Since we still cannot use the negative root in this problem, the answer is 3 seconds.

7. We will use the same formula for vertical motion that we are growing to know and love so well: $y = \left(-\frac{1}{2}\right)gx^2 + v_0x + h$. In this problem, we know x (the time is given to us in the problem as 5 seconds). We know g is the acceleration due to gravity, and we know two constants for this acceleration. Since we haven't done much with the metric system of measurements, let's use $g = 9.8$ meters/sec². (Just for rough estimation, a meter is a little bit longer than a yard.) We know that h, the initial height, is the same at the beginning and at the end, so we can set $h = 0$, since there is no change. We also know that $y = 0$ when the stuffed critter is caught. So, do we know everything except v_0? Almost. Let's substitute our known values into the formula and find it:

Let $0 = \left(-\frac{1}{2}\right)(9.8)(25) + v_0(5) + 0$. Simplifying a bit, we have $0 = -122.5 + 5v_0$, and $5v_0 = 122.5$, so $v_0 = 24.5$. The initial velocity was 24.5 meters per second.

How can we check this? Simple. Let's say that, if we know the initial velocity is 24.5 meters per second, when will the stuffed creature be at height 0? Using the same constant for acceleration, we have:

$y = \left(-\frac{1}{2}\right)gx^2 + v_0x + h = \left(-\frac{1}{2}\right)(9.8)x^2 + 24.5x + 0 = -(4.9)x^2 + 24.5x$.

We want to find x when $y = 0$, so we set $-(4.9)x^2 + 24.5x = 0$ and think quadratic formula with $a = -4.9$, $b = 24.5$ and $c = 0$.

First, the discriminant: $b^2 - 4ac = 24.5^2 - 4(-4.9)(0) = 24.5^2$.

Now, the quadratic formula:

$$x = \frac{-b \pm \sqrt{b^2 - 4ac}}{2a}$$

$$= \frac{-24.5 \pm \sqrt{24.5^2}}{2(-4.9)}$$

$$= \frac{-24.5 \pm 24.5}{-9.8}$$

$$= 0, 5$$

So, when the initial velocity is 24.5 meters per second, the tossed object is at height 0 at 0 and 5 seconds, exactly as our problem stated.

8. To solve this problem, we have to find the speed that will let the braking distance be equal to 25 feet. Then, we'll be able to say that they can drive at any speed less than that and still brake to a stop before they crash into the tuba players.

So, since d is the braking distance, we set $d = 25$ feet and solve for v, like this:

Let $d = 25 = v + \frac{v^2}{15}$. Multiply each side of the equation by 15 to make things simpler. The $15(25) = 15v + v^2$, so, putting this in standard form, $v^2 + 15v - 375 = 0$, and we have a quadratic equation in standard form, where $a = 1$, $b = 15$, and $c = -375$. It really doesn't look like factoring will work here, so we turn to our great pal, solver of many mysteries, the quadratic formula:

First, the discriminant:

$$b^2 - 4ac = 15^2 - 4(1)(-375) = 225 + 1500 = 1725$$

Now, the quadratic formula:

$$x = \frac{-b \pm \sqrt{b^2 - 4ac}}{2a}$$

$$= \frac{-15 \pm \sqrt{1,725}}{2(1)}$$

$$\approx \frac{-15 \pm 41.5}{2}$$

$$\approx 13.25, \; -28.25$$

Once again, we cannot use the negative root, so the float can be driven at speeds up to about 13.25 feet per second and still brake within 25 feet of the marching band.

To give us a better perspective on this speed, the problem asks that we convert it to miles per hour, which we do as follows:

$$\left[\frac{13.25 \text{ feet}}{1 \text{ second}}\right]\left[\frac{1 \text{ mile}}{5,280 \text{ feet}}\right]\left[\frac{3,600 \text{ seconds}}{1 \text{ hour}}\right] = \frac{47,700 \text{ miles}}{5,280 \text{ hours}}$$

$$\approx 9.0 \text{ miles per hour}$$

Since the band probably can't hit this speed marching, the float drivers will be more likely to be travelling around 4 miles per hour or less and will have plenty of braking distance.

9. For this problem, we have an equation that tells us how to find the weight as a function of altitude and we are asked to find the altitude at which $W = 10$. So, since the equation is not in simplified form, we will first simplify it, then set it equal to 10, then solve it, as follows:

$$W = 145\left(\frac{6,400}{6,400 + x}\right)^2$$

$$= \frac{145(6,400)^2}{(6,400 + x)^2}$$

$$= \frac{145(6,400)^2}{6,400^2 + 2(6,400)(x) + x^2}$$

$$= \frac{(145)(40,960,000)}{40,960,000 + 12,800x + x^2}$$

So, let $W = 10 = \dfrac{(145)(40,960,000)}{40,960,000 + 12,800x + x^2}$

Then, $(10)(40,960,000 + 12,800x + x^2) = (145)(40,960,000)$

And $40,960,000 + 12,800x + x^2 \dfrac{(145)(40,960,000)}{10}$

$= 593,920,000$

Rearranging, we have $x^2 + 12,800x + 40,960,000 = 593,920,000$

So $x^2 - 12,800x - 552,960,000 = 0$.

Aha! A quadratic equation (surprise)!

So now, $a = 1$, $b = 12,800$, and $c = -552,960,000$

First, the discriminant: $b^2 - 4ac = 12,800^2 - 4(1)(-552,960,000)$

$= 163,840,000 + 2,211,840,000 = 2,375,680,000$

- What did one mushroom say to the other?

- You're a fungi to be with.

Now, the quadratic formula:

$$x = \frac{-b \pm \sqrt{b^2 - 4ac}}{2a}$$

$$= \frac{-12,800 \pm \sqrt{2,375,680,000}}{2(1)}$$

$$\approx \frac{-12,800 \pm 48,740.9}{2}$$

$$\approx 17,970.5, \; -21,785.2$$

Once again, we cannot use the negative root in this problem, because the formula holds only for altitudes above the Earth's surface, so the answer is that the passenger will weigh 10 pounds at an altitude of about 17,970.5 feet.

10. We must haul out our trusty formula for vertical motion, noticing that there is an initial velocity in this problem of 40 feet per second. So, what we will start with is $y = \left(-\frac{1}{2}\right)gx^2 + v_0 x + h$, with $g = 32$ ft/sec^2 (since the units have to match or the problem will be wrong), $v_0 = 40$ ft/sec, and y and h are both equal to 0 (actually, they could both be equal to 1 or 10 or 4,000. The important thing is that they are the same number, since the rocket started and ended at the same place).

Substituting, we have $y = 0 = \left(-\frac{1}{2}\right)(32)x^2 + 40x$, so $0 = -16x^2 + 40x$.

This is pretty easy to factor, like so: $0 = -8x(2x - 5)$

Then, setting each factor to zero and solving, we have $-8x = 0$, so $x = 0$. Then, $2x - 5 = 0$, so $x = \frac{5}{2}$ and our roots will be $0, \frac{5}{2}$.

What this means in terms of this problem is that the flight started from the ground at $x = 0$ and ended back on the ground and $x = \frac{5}{2}$ seconds, so the flight lasted for $\frac{5}{2} - 0 = \frac{5}{2}$ seconds.

11. This problem describes another case of vertical motion, so we will model the situation using $y = -(\frac{1}{2})gx^2 + v_0x + h$. Once again, the units in the problem are in feet, so we must use $g = 32$ ft/sec^2. Since the turkey is dropped, not thrown with any additional velocity up OR down, the initial velocity is 0 and $v_0x = 0$ for all x. The initial height is given as 4 feet, so $h = 4$, while the height at which the turkey is caught is $4 - 2 = 2$ feet, so $y = 2$. Then, substituting, we have:

$$y = \left(-\frac{1}{2}\right)gx^2 + v_0x + h$$

$$2 = \left(-\frac{1}{2}\right)(32)x^2 + 0 + 4$$

$$-2 = -16x^2$$

$$\frac{1}{8} = x^2$$

$$\sqrt{\frac{1}{8}} = x.$$

The negative square root has no meaning in the context of this problem, since the turkey is dropped at $x = 0$ seconds and time does not run backwards on THIS Earth (not yet, anyway) so, using a calculator to find the square root of 0.125, the cat has about 0.3535 second.

The cat will tire of the game and waddle away only after it has eaten as much turkey as it can possibly hold.

12. No more than five times. Remember that the degree of any polynomial indicates the maximum number of times that the curve of the polynomial can cross any horizontal line.

13. a. $(x + 3)(x - 2) = x^2 +$ ___   **First terms**

$= x^2 + (-2x) +$ ___   **Outer terms**

$= x^2 + (-2x) + 3x +$ ___   **Inner terms**

$= x^2 + (-2x) + 3x + (-6)$ **Last terms**

$= x^2 + x - 6$ **Collect like terms**

b. $(x - 3)(y - 2) = xy + \underline{\quad}$ **First terms**

$= xy + (-2x) + \underline{\quad}$ **Outer terms**

$= xy + (-2x) + (-3y) + \underline{\quad}$ **Inner terms**

$= xy + (-2x) + (-3y) + 6$ **Last terms**

$= xy - 2x - 3y + 6$ **There are no like terms.**

c. $(x - 3)(x - 3) = x^2 + \underline{\quad}$ **First terms**

$= x^2 + (-3x) + \underline{\quad}$ **Outer terms**

$= x^2 + (-3x) + (-3x) + \underline{\quad}$ **Inner terms**

$= x^2 + (-3x) + (-3x) + 9$ **Last terms**

$= x^2 - 6x + 9$ **Collect like terms**

$\underline{\qquad}$ or $\underline{\qquad}$

d. $(x + 4)(x + 2) = x^2 + $ ____ **First terms**

$= x^2 + 2x + $ ____ **Outer terms**

$= x^2 + 2x + 4x + $ ____ **Inner terms**

$= x^2 + 2x + 4x + 8$ **Last terms**

$= x^2 + 6x + 8$ **Collect like terms**

e. $(2x - 1)(x + 1) = 2x^2 + $ ____ **First terms**

$= 2x^2 + 2x + $ ____ **Outer terms**

$= 2x^2 + 2x + (-1x) + $ ____ **Inner terms**

$= 2x^2 + 2x + (-1x) + (-1)$ **Last terms**

$= 2x^2 + x - 1$ **Collect like terms**

f. $(3x - y)(x + 2y) = 3x^2 +$ ____   **First terms**

$= 3x^2 + 6xy +$ ____   **Outer terms**

$= 3x^2 + 6xy + (-xy) +$ ____   **Inner terms**

$= 3x^2 + 6xy + (-xy) + (-2y^2)$ **Last terms**

$= 3x^2 + 5xy - 2y^2$ **Collect like terms**

g. $(2p - q)(3p - 2q) = 6p^2 +$ ____   **First terms**

$= 6p^2 + (-4pq) +$ ____   **Outer terms**

$= 6p^2 + (-4pq) + (-3pq) +$ ____   **Inner terms**

$= 6p^2 + (-4pq) + (-3pq) + 2q^2$ **Last terms**

$= 6p^2 - 7pq + 2q^2$ **Collect like terms**

h. $(2m - 3n)(2m + 3q) = 4m^2 +$ ___   **First terms**

$= 4m^2 + 6mq +$ ___   **Outer terms**

$= 4m^2 + 6mq + (-6mn) +$ ___ **Inner terms**

$= 4m^2 + 6mq - 6mn + (-9nq)$ **Last terms**

$= 4m^2 + 6mq - 6mn - 9nq$

14. a. $(x^2)(3xy^4) = 3(x)(x^2)y^4$

$= 3x^{1+2}y^4$

$= 3x^3y^4$

b. $(2p + q)(3r) = 6pr + 3qr$

c. $(2x + y)(3r)^2 = (2x + y)(9r^2)$

$= 18r^2x + 9r^2y$

d. $(2m + n)^2(3r) = [4m^2 + (2)(2m)(n) + n^2](3r)$

$= (4m^2 + 4mn + n^2)(3r)$

$= 12m^2r + 12mnr + 3n^2r$

e. $(2x + y)^3(3p) = (3p)[(2x + y)(2x + y)^2]$

$= (3p)[(2x + y)(4x^2 + 4xy + y^2)]$

$= (3p)[(2x)(4x^2 + 4xy + y^2) + (y)(4x^2 + 4xy + y^2)]$

$= (3p)(8x^3 + 8x^2y + 2xy^2 + 4x^2y + 4xy^2 + y^3)$

$= (3p)(8x^3 + 12x^2y + 6xy^2 + y^3)$

$= 24px^3 + 36px^2y + 18pxy^2 + 3py^3$

15. a. $x^2 - 3x + 2 = (x - 1)(x - 2)$

How did we do that? Trial and error. First, we noticed that the possible factors for the first term were 1 and 1 OR −1 and −1. Then, we noticed that the possible factors for the third term were 1 and 2 OR −1 and −2. Since the sign of the middle term is negative, we can choose $(x - ?)(x - ?)$ OR $(-x + ?)(-x + ?)$.

We like to use the simplest possible variables, so, choosing $(x - ?)(x - ?)$, we only have one choice for the constant terms: -1 and -2.

But, if we wanted to use $(-x + ?)(-x + ?)$, we would use the positive constant terms to get factors of $(-x + 1)(-x + 2)$, which is also correct.

b. $m^2 + 2m + 1 = (m + 1)(m + 1) = (m + 1)^2$

How did we do that? Two ways. The first way, trial and error, is done by noticing that the possible factors for the first term were 1 and 1 OR -1 and -1. Then, we noticed that the possible factors for the second term were also 1 and 1 OR -1 and -1. Then we noticed the positive sign for the middle term, so we knew we could choose between $(m + 1)(m + 1)$ or $(-m - 1)(-m - 1)$. Both are correct, but we liked the first better because it is simpler.

The second way is by noticing the pattern: The first and last terms are perfect squares, and the middle term is twice the product of the first and last terms. Since we recall that is the pattern of a perfect square trinomial, we factor it by taking the square roots of the first and last terms and inserting the sign of the middle term between them.

c. $x^3 - 8y^3 = (x - 2y)(x^2 + 2xy + 4y^2)$

This problem can also be done in two ways. Both ways start by requiring us to notice that the two terms are each perfect cubes (of x and $-2y$, respectively). The first way then requires that we remember the pattern for factoring the difference of two cubes (which is in the Other Important Stuff section of this workbook) and just write down the answer.

The second way is by thinking that $(x - 2y)$ is probably one factor of the polynomial, so, if it is, we can just divide it into $x^3 - 8y^3$ to see what the other factor is. And we do that this way:

$$
\begin{array}{r}
x^2 + 2xy + 4y^2 \\
x - 2y \overline{)x^3 + 0x^2y + 0xy^2 - 8y^3} \\
\underline{x^3 - 2x^2y} \\
+ 2x^2y + 0xy^2 \\
\underline{+ 2x^2y - 4xy^2} \\
+ 4xy^2 - 8y^3 \\
\underline{+ 4xy^2 - 8y^3} \\
0
\end{array}
$$

Remember, when you're factoring, you can always fall back on polynomial division if you can guess one factor, although it is kind of the hard way to do things. Then, we look at $x^2 + 2xy + 4y^2$ and find no pairs of factors for the first and last terms that will give us the middle term, so we are done.

d. $144x^2 - 169 = (12x + 13)(12x - 13)$

This expression we recognize as the difference of perfect squares, so the factorization is very easy, done by the rule.

e. $25b^2 + 4$ cannot be factored.

Remember that only the difference of perfect squares can be factored.

f. $9 - (x^5 - 3x + p)^2 = (3 + x^5 - 3x + p)[3 - (x^5 - 3x + p)]$

$$= (3 + x^5 - 3x + p)(3 - x^5 + 3x - p)$$

This expression is also the difference of two perfect squares, and so it's factored by the rule. The second factor needs to be simplified before the calculation is complete.

16. a. Here is the graph and table of values for $y = -x^2$:

table values

x	y
0	0
1	-1
-1	-1
2	-4
-2	-4
3	-9
-3	-9

graph

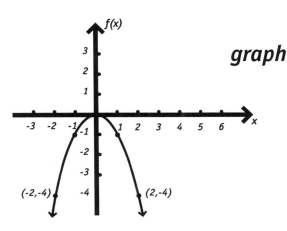

b. Here is the graph and table of values for $y = \frac{1}{4}x^2$

table values

x	y
0	0
1	1/4
-1	1/4
2	1
-2	1
4	4
-4	4

graph

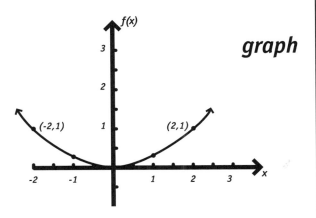

c. Here is the graph and table of values for $y = x^2 + 4x + 4$:

table values

graph

x	y
0	4
1	9
-1	1
-2	0
-3	1
-4	4
-5	9

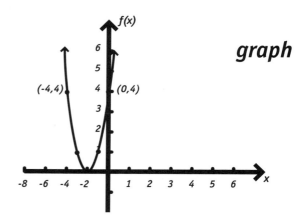

d. Here is the graph and table of values for $y = -x^2 + 2x - 1$:

table values

graph

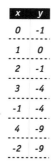

x	y
0	-1
1	0
2	-1
3	-4
-1	-4
4	-9
-2	-9

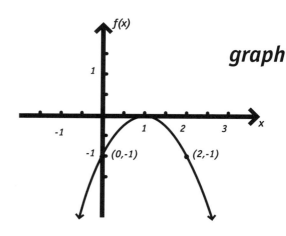

e. Here is the graph and table of values for $y = -x^2 - 2x + 3$:

table values

x	y
0	3
1	0
-1	4
-2	3
-3	0
2	-5
-4	-5

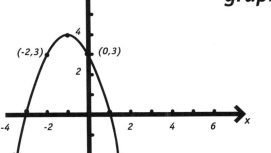

graph

17. a. $(x - 2)^2 = 9$ means that $(x - 2)(x - 2) = 9$, or
$x^2 - 2x - 2x + 4 = 9$, so we combine like terms to
get $x^2 - 4x - 5 = 0$.

Now, looking at this equation, we might be able to factor it
easily. Possible firsts would be $(1x)(1x)$ and $(-1x)(-1x)$, and
possible lasts would be $(-1)(5)$ and $(1)(-5)$. Since 1 and -5
would add up to -4, we factor and get

$(x + 1)(x - 5) = 0$

So, if $x + 1 = 0$, $x = -1$ and if $x - 5 = 0$, $x = 5$. Therefore,
the roots of this equation are -1 and 5.

Checking by substituting into the original equation, we see that:

$$[(-1) - 2]^2 = (-3)^2 = 9 \text{ and } (5 - 2)^2 = (3)^2 = 9.$$

b. $(m + 1)^2 - 8 = 0$ means that, recalling the pattern for squaring a binomial,

$$m^2 + 2(m)(1) + 12 - 8 = 0$$

Combining like terms, we get

$$m^2 + 2m - 7 = 0.$$

Now, since the possible firsts are $(1m)(1m)$ and $(-1m)(-1m)$, while possible lasts would be $(-1)(7)$ and $(1)(-7)$, and there is just no way any combination of these will add up to $2m$, we must resort to the quadratic formula.

So, since $a = 1$, $b = 2$, and $c = -7$, the discriminant is

$$b^2 - 4ac = 2^2 - (4)(1)(-7) = 4 + 28 = 32.$$

Then, using the quadratic formula, we have:

$$x = \frac{-b \pm \sqrt{b^2 - 4ac}}{2a}$$

$$= \frac{-2 \pm \sqrt{32}}{2(1)}$$

$$= \frac{-2 \pm 4\sqrt{2}}{2}$$

$$= -1 \pm 2\sqrt{2}$$

The roots are $x = -1 - 2\sqrt{2}$ and $-1 + 2\sqrt{2}$. You can practice your algebra skills by substituting these into the original equation, one at a time, to check that they are correct.

c. $x^2 - x = 12$ means that $x^2 - x - 12 = 0$.

Now, looking at this equation, we might be able to factor it easily. Possible firsts would be $(1x)(1x)$ and $(-1x)(-1x)$, and possible lasts would be $(-1)(12)$, $(1)(-12)$, $(-2)(6)$, $(2)(-6)$, $(-3)(4)$ and $(-4)(3)$. Since -4 and 3 would add up to -1, we factor and get:

$$(x - 4)(x + 3) = 0$$

So, if $x - 4 = 0$, $x = 4$ and if $x + 3 = 0$, $x = -3$. Therefore, the roots of this equation are -3 and 4.

d. $m^2 + 4m + 1 = 0$ doesn't look much like a candidate for factoring because the firsts and lasts will be 1 or -1 (with or without the m) and there is no way we can make a middle term of $4m$ out of that. So, we will go directly to the quadratic formula, with $a = 1$, $b = 4$, and $c = 1$ (because the equation is already in standard form).

First, the discriminant: $b^2 - 4ac = 4^2 - 4(1)(1) = 12$.

Now, the quadratic formula:

$$x = \frac{-b \pm \sqrt{b^2 - 4ac}}{2a}$$

$$= \frac{-4 \pm \sqrt{12}}{2(1)}$$

$$= \frac{-4 \pm 2\sqrt{3}}{2}$$

$$= -2 \pm \sqrt{3}$$

The roots are $x = -2 - \sqrt{3}$ and $-2 + \sqrt{3}$.

e. $p^2 + 6 = 0$ means that $p^2 = -6$, so $p = \pm\sqrt{-6} = \pm\sqrt{6}\sqrt{-1} = \pm\sqrt{6}i$

The roots are $x = \sqrt{6}i$ and $\sqrt{-6}i$.

Matho Searcho Solution

Matho Crosso Solution

297

The Other Matho Searcho Solution

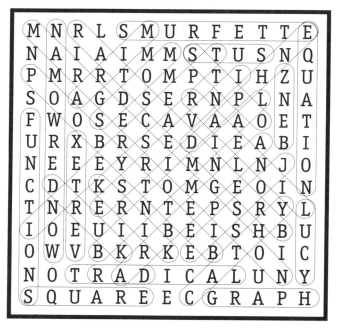

The Other Matho Crosso Solution

GLOSSARY

algebra - A field of mathematics that studies real numbers and the operations of addition, subtraction, multiplication, and division using symbols and numbers.

algebraic properties - A set of rules that define algebra and tell you how to manipulate numbers and symbols when doing algebra problems. The algebraic properties are discussed in the **VIDEO NOTES** and are listed in **OTHER IMPORTANT STUFF**.

arithmetic - A field of mathematics that studies real numbers and the operations of addition, subtraction, multiplication, and division.

axis of symmetry - The straight line that passes through the middle of a curve so that it cuts the curve into two mirror-images. For a parabola, if its equation is $y = ax^2 + bx + c$, the axis of symmetry is the line:

$$x = \frac{-b}{2a}.$$

binomial - A function or expression that contains exactly two terms. $f(x) = ax + b$ is a binomial function. Another example is $f(x) = 5x^2 + 7x$.

bow tie pasta - Pasta shaped like a bow tie. Commonly served with fancy cream sauces.

Burgas - Fifth largest city in Bulgaria, with a population of 182,570 (monetary unit is the lev).

complex numbers - Numbers that consist of two parts: real and imaginary. They take the form of $a + bi$, where a and b are real numbers and $i = \sqrt{-1}$.

constant - A value that does not change. Constants are usually written as real numbers. If they are not known, they are often symbolized by a, b, c, and k. Pi is a famous constant that is symbolized by a Greek letter.

coordinate plane - A plane on which a coordinate system has been imagined to exist so that it's possible to graph functions. The coordinate plane used in basic Algebra is known as the rectangular, or Cartesian, coordinate plane, and consists of a plane upon which two lines (called axes, pronounced "ax-eez") cross each other, forming right angles at their intersection. The horizontal axis is the x-axis and the vertical axis is the y-axis. The intersection of the axes (called the origin) is considered to be the zero-point for each axis, with positive numbers proceeding from the origin to the right along the x-axis and from the origin up the page along the y-axis. Negative numbers proceed to the left of the origin in a mirror-image along the x-axis, and proceed down the page from the origin, in a mirror image, along the y-axis. The distances between the positive and negative number-marks along an axis is always the same.

degree - The highest exponent on any term in a polynomial. For example, $x + 2$ is of degree 1, and $x^2 + 2$ is of degree 2. The polynomial $x^4 + x + 2$ is of degree 4. The polynomial $x + 24$ is of degree 1 because you ignore the exponent of the constant when you determine the degree of the polynomial.

dependent variable - A variable whose value is determined by the value of the independent variable. For example, let $y = f(x) = 2x$. The dependent variable is y, or $f(x)$. The independent variable is x. You have to choose an x to find the dependent variable y for that x.

discriminant - The name of a portion of the quadratic formula which tells you what kind of roots the equation has. The discriminant is $b^2 + 4ac$. If it is > 0, the equation has two real roots. If it is $= 0$, the equation has one real root. If it is < 0, the equation has NO real roots (instead it has imaginary or complex roots).

domain - The domain of a function is the set of values that can be used for the independent variable.

equation - A statement that indicates equality between two mathematical expressions, often by the use of the equal sign, "$=$."

evaluate - A function is evaluated by substituting values for the variables and then performing the indicated operations. It basically means "doing" the equation.

exponent - A symbol that is written above and to the right of another symbol or number to indicate repeated multiplication in basic algebra. It is also called a "power."

factor - An expression that multiplies another expression. The factors in the equation $(x - 4)(x + 3) + 2x - 5 = 0$ are $(x - 4)$ and $(x + 3)$. Used as a verb, "to factor" means to find the expressions which, when multiplied together, result in another expression.

function - A rule that associates each element of one set (the domain of the function) with one and only one element of another set (the range of the function). Also an event where Brie cheese is served.

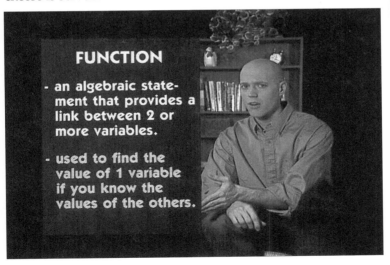

FUNCTION

- an algebraic statement that provides a link between 2 or more variables.

- used to find the value of 1 variable if you know the values of the others.

geometry - A field of mathematics that studies the measurement, properties, and relationships between points, lines, angles, planes, and solids.

giraffe - Known as *Giraffa camelopardalis tippelskirchi*, giraffes are ruminate ungulates. An adult male can reach a height of 18 feet and weigh as much as 3,000 pounds. Giraffes can also eat up to 75 pounds of acacia leaves per day and drink 10 gallons of water. The hairs in a giraffe's tail are 20 times thicker than human hairs.

graph - A special visual representation of a mathematical relation, or the process of creating such a representation. Graphs show the solution of the relation pictorially and are made with reference to coordinate systems, the most common of which is the rectangular or Cartesian coordinate system.

imaginary numbers - Numbers that are not real and do not exist on the real number line. They take the form of *bi*, where *b* is a real number and $i = \sqrt{-1}$.

independent variable - A variable that does not depend on the value of any other variable. For functions in standard form, the independent variable is the only variable in the expression to the right of the equals sign.

inequality - A statement that two mathematical expressions are NOT equal (contrast with equation). The symbols used for inequality are "<," meaning "less than," and ">," meaning "greater than." In each case, the symbol points to the smaller quantity, so we can say that $1 < 10$ or $x + y > 42$. You can also think of the open side as an alligator about to swallow the bigger quantity.

infinity - A mathematical concept that has no real equivalent on earth. Something that has no end, that cannot be described by a real number and that is either very, very, very, very, very, very large or very, very, very, very, very, very small.

intercept - The point (or points) at which an axis is crossed. The y-intercept is a point at which $x = 0$ for any equation, but the x-intercept (or root) is a point where $y = 0$ for any equation. A function may have only one y-intercept at most, but many x-intercepts.

inverse function - One of a pair of functions that has the effect of undoing the operations of the other function. An inverse function does not exist by itself, but only as part of a pair of functions. If $f(x) = 2x$, then the inverse function, called $g(x)$, is $g(x) = \frac{f(x)}{2}$ So if $x = 2, f(x) = 4$, then $g(x) = \frac{4}{2} = 2$.

irrational - A number that cannot be written as a real fraction. Examples of irrational numbers are π, $\sqrt{2}$, $\sqrt{3}$, and $\sqrt{5}$.

lasagna - Long, flat, pasta noodles, usually served in layers with cheese and meat.

linear equation - An equation in which no variable is multiplied by another variable (or itself) in its simplest form. A linear equation is any equation of degree (or order) one. $2x + 3y = 2$ is a linear equation. $2xy = 3$ is not a linear equation. $2x^2 = 4$ is not a linear equation.

macaroni - Small, elbow–shaped pasta often served with lots of cheese.

monocle - A lens for one eye. Popular many decades ago; they fell out of use because of the difficulty people had in wearing them.

monomial - A function or expression that contains only one term. $f(x) = x$ is a monomial function.

operation - A defined mathematical action typically performed on one or two numbers or variables such as addition, subtraction, multiplication, and division. Also a method of curing an ingrown toenail.

ossicones - Commonly referred to as "horns" on a giraffe. They are in fact not true horns, but merely bony protuberances on top of the giraffe head used for fighting with other giraffes (hey, don't mess with a giraffe).

order - Just another name for the degree of a polynomial.

ordered pair - A pair of numbers written in a specific order within parentheses. In basic algebra, ordered pairs are written with the value of the independent variable first, followed by the value of the dependent variable, like this: (x, y), $(1, 2)$, $(0, 0)$.

Paucek - A dysfunctional family from Florida with severe problems. But they're very nice, and their youngest son started Cerebellum.

parabola - The name of the curve that is produced by graphing quadratic equations of the form $y = ax^2 + bx + c$, where a, b, and c are real numbers and $a \neq 0$.

perfect square trinomial - An expression that can be factored so easily, it's a treat. Its first and last terms are perfect squares (e.g., x^2, 4, $16y^2$) and its middle term is twice the product of the square roots of the first and last terms. Learn to recognize these in your sleep. They save time (which is money), AND wear 'n tear on the old brain.

point - A one-dimensional object. In the rectangular, or Cartesian, coordinate system, a point is located on the graph by an ordered pair (x, y) that tells how far it is from the x-axis and how far it is from the y-axis. Two points determine a line.

point-slope form - A common and useful way of representing a straight line. Representing the slope by m and a known point by (x_1, y_1), the point-slope form is:

$$y - y_1 = m(x - x_1).$$

polynomial - A mathematical expression or function containing two or more terms. $x^7 + 3x^2 - 4$ is a polynomial expression; $f(x) = 4x - 16$ is a polynomial function.

power - An exponent that indicates the number of times a number or variable is multiplied by itself, in the case of whole numbers used as powers. In the function $y = x^2$, the power of x is 2.

primavera - A pasta dish of pasta noodles and lots of spring vegetables.

quadratic equation - An equation in which any variable is multiplied by another variable (or itself) only once in its simplest form. A quadratic equation is any equation of degree (or order) two. $3x^2 + 4x = 7$ and $2x^2 = 4$ are quadratic equations. $2x^2y = 0$ and $2x^3 = 4$ are not quadratic equations.

quadratic formula - Formula that allows you to find the roots of a quadratic equation that is otherwise impossible to factor.

$$x = \frac{-b \pm \sqrt{b^2 - 4ac}}{2a}$$

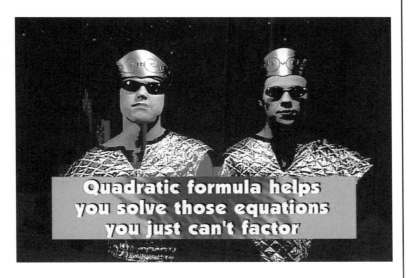

radical - In mathematics, the symbol for taking a root: $\sqrt{a}$. The root for the word "radical" is *radix*, which is Latin for "root," and which is also the root for the word "radish."

rational - Any real number that can be put in the form $\frac{a}{b}$, where *a* and *b* are whole numbers.

real numbers - Numbers that have no imaginary part. Examples of real numbers are 10, .800, $\frac{1}{3}$, and π.

range - The set of values that can be obtained as the function processes the values in its domain. It is the set of values that the dependent variable can take on.

relation - A mathematical connection between two sets (both of numbers, or one of a variable and one of numbers, for example). A relation is the most general form of this connection. All functions are relations, all inequalities are relations, all equations are relations, but not all relations are functions.

rigatoni - Small, ridged, tube-shaped pasta.

risotto - Short-grained Italian rice.

rise - The vertical distance between any two points on a line.

root - Any point where the function's graph crosses the x-axis or any x where $y = f(x) = 0$. An x-intercept is a root. For quadratic and some other classes of equations, the curve does not cross the x-axis, so the values of x for which $y = 0$ are called imaginary roots.

I thought that spleen was a spitting image of my brother's.

-Fletch

ruminant ungulate - Hoof-stock herbivorous animal, such as a giraffe or gazelle.

run - The horizontal distance between any two points on a line.

set - A collection of objects that is formed using some rule, which can be simple or complex. For example, the set of negative numbers is all the real numbers that are less than zero.

Setswana - The official language of the country of Botswana.

slope - A measure of the inclination of a line. The ratio of the rise over the run for any two points on a line is its slope.

slope-intercept form - A common and useful way of representing a straight line. Using m to symbolize slope and b to symbolize the y-intercept, the point-slope form of a line is given by:

$$y = mx + b.$$

spaghetti - Long, thin pasta noodles...a very common pasta.

square - To multiply something by itself once.

standard form (of a function) - A function is in standard form if it is written in the form of $y = f(x)$.

$$y = ax^2 + bx + c.$$

term - A number or the product of a number and one or more variables. Individual terms are separated by $+$ or $-$ signs. Examples of terms are 5, x, $5x$, and $5xy$.

trinomial - A function or expression that contains exactly three terms. $f(x) = 9x^5 + 7x + 13$ is a trinomial function.

triskaidekaphobia - Fear of the number 13.

variable - A non numeric symbol that can take on more than one value. Unknown variables, those whose values are to be solved by the algebraic manipulation of equations, are usually written as x, y, z, but may be any symbol.

vertex - The midpoint of the curve of a parabola, at the place on the curve where the curve intersects its axis of symmetry and where its direction changes from positive to negative (or negative to positive). If the equation of the parabola is given by $y = ax^2 + bx + c$, the vertex is found at

$$\left(\frac{-b}{2a}, \frac{-b^2 + 4ac}{4a} \right)$$

x-intercept - The point(s) at which a curve crosses the x-axis. It is found by setting $y = 0$ and solving for x.

y-intercept - The point(s) at which a curve crosses the y-axis. It is found by setting $x = 0$ and solving for y. For polynomial equations in standard form, the constant term is the y-intercept.

NOTES

NOTES

NOTES

NOTES

319

STUDY SIDEKICK

NOTES

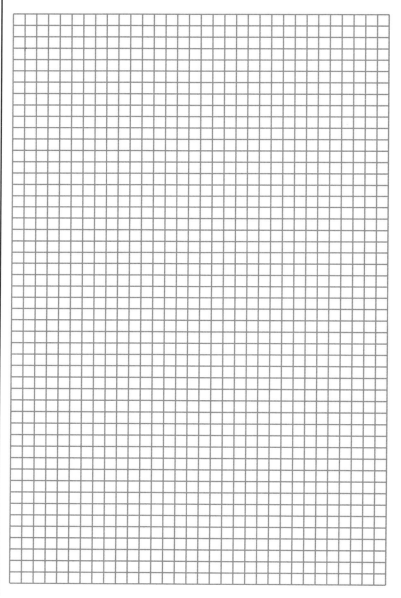

GRAPH PAPER

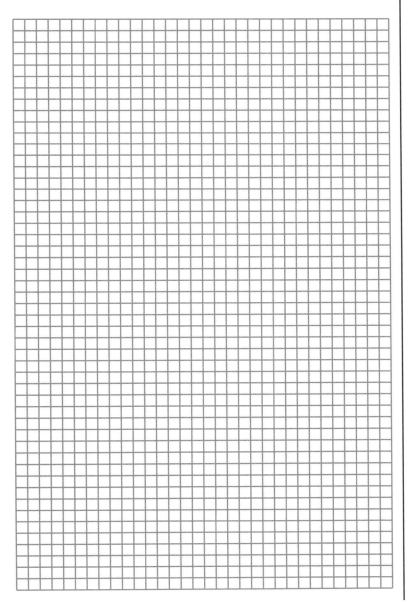

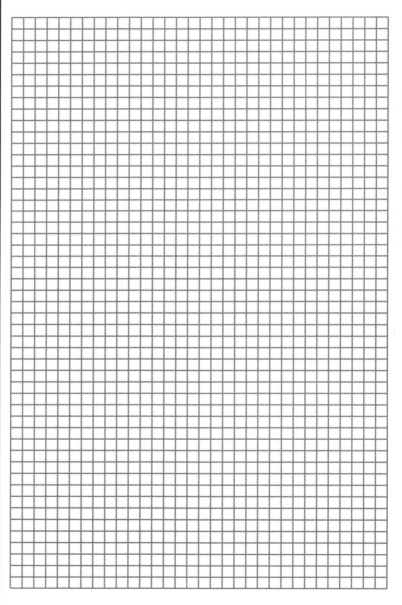

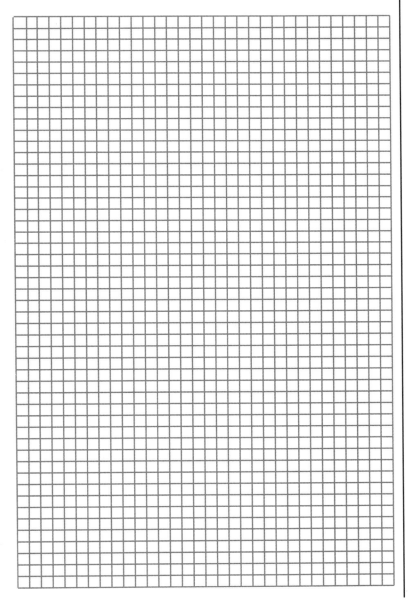

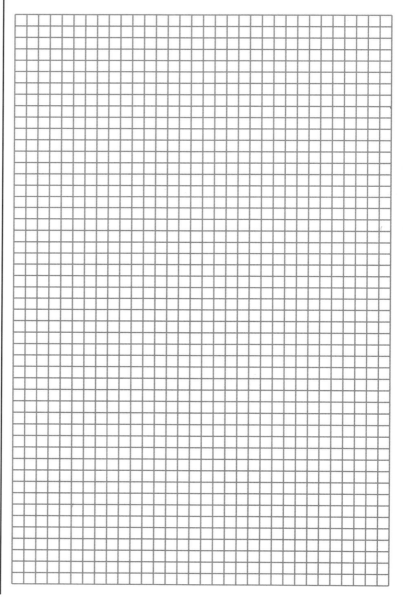